A History of Canadian Journalism, Volume 1

Canadian Press Association

GOLDWIN SMITH, D.C.L.

O

A HISTORY

OF

CANADIAN JOURNALISM

IN THE

SEVERAL PORTIONS OF THE DOMINION

WITH A

SKETCH

OF THE

CANADIAN PRESS ASSOCIATION

1859–1908

EDITED BY A COMMITTEE OF THE ASSOCIATION

TORONTO
1908

in
of
wa
thi
int
for
ide
ma
Gc
pri
at
in
of
sur
all
]
As
det
sur
for
this
be
cel
soc

PREFACE

WHEN it was resolved to celebrate the fiftieth anniversary of the Canadian Press Association in 1908, the wish was expressed that a literary memorial of a permanent character should be prepared. The duty was entrusted to a small committee, and the result is this volume, which, it is hoped, will prove of some interest and value to a community wider than that formed by members of the Press. That the original idea was to include purely literary as well as historical material, may be inferred from the contributions of Mr. Goldwin Smith and Mr. J. W. Bengough. But this proved too ambitious an undertaking with the resources at command. The volume, therefore, is chiefly historical in its scope, and aims to present not merely a narrative of the proceedings of the Association, but a general survey of the establishment and growth of the Press in all parts of Canada.

In compiling the records of the Canadian Press Association, it was considered advisable to dwell in some detail upon the earlier history of the organization, summarizing briefly the later period, which is already set forth in the elaborate annual reports now in print. For this reason the proceedings of the meeting for 1908 must be sought in the report which was issued after the celebration. The preparation of a history of the Association was much facilitated by Mr. Wm. Buckingham, Mr. Richard White, the late Mr. John Cameron, Mr. David Creighton, Mr. R. Sellar, Miss Gillespy of Hamilton; Mr. H. B. Donly, Mr. W. M. O'Beirne, Mr. A. T. Wilgress, Mr. M. A. James, Mr. E. J. B. Pense, Mr. H. F. Gardiner, Mr. T. H. Preston, Mr. J. A. Cooper, Mr. C. D. Barr, Mr. C. J. Bowell and others, who either by the production of records and documents hitherto inaccessible, or by drawing upon personal recollection, made it possible to reconstruct the story of the past. For this valuable assistance, so cheerfully rendered, the Committee is especially grateful.

The articles dealing with the Press by Provinces furnish a comprehensive survey of the development of journalism in Canada. Of the birth of the first Canadian paper in 1752, and of subsequent journalistic events in the Maritime Provinces, Mr. J. E. B. McCready, Charlottetown, writes; Mr. John Reade, F.R.S.C., Montreal, contributes a scholarly article on the trend of journalism as illustrated in Quebec; Mr. Arthur Wallis, Toronto, writes of Ontario; Messrs. J. P. Robertson, Winnipeg; J. K. McInnis, Regina, and R. E. Gosnell, Vancouver, of the West, where journalism has more history, particularly in British Columbia, than might be supposed, and to these is added a short reminiscent article by Mr. Robert Sellar, Huntingdon, Que. To these gentlemen the Committee wishes to express its indebtedness, an indebtedness which, it is felt, will be shared by every Canadian connected with the Press. Their work supplies a record of journalism which, it is believed, will take rank with the best Canadian history and biography.

The Committee wishes, too, to express its thanks to Mr. H. C. Bell for exceedingly valuable assistance in correcting and revising the proofs.

The promise of the late Hon. J. I. Tarte to contribute an article on the French Press was frustrated by the hand of death, and to this extent the book is incomplete. One other phase of Canadian journalism which is left for a future historian is a sketch of the Parliamentary Press Galleries. The Committee also had prepared a Chronology of the Canadian Press, covering the entire period from 1752 to 1908, but this grew to such voluminous proportions that it was found impossible to include it in the present book.

JOHN R. BONE,
JOSEPH T. CLARK.
A. H. U. COLQUHOUN.
JOHN F. MACKAY.

TORONTO, 1908.

TABLE OF CONTENTS

THE JOURNALISTIC FELLOWSHIP.

1859—1908.

IN honor of our golden year,
  In honor of the tie that binds
  In unity our hearts and minds,
Accept this grateful souvenir.

Herein is told once more the tale
  Of Fellowship's enduring might
  To aid the cause of Peace and Right
Where honor and good faith prevail.

For half-a-century we've stood—
  Whate'er the strain of party ties,
  Or diverse creeds and sympathies,
A firm and genial Brotherhood;

Progressing ever more and more
  In material service each to each,
  And ever finding kindlier speech
To shame the ranc'rous days of yore.

Here truce is called; the venom'd pen
  Is dropped, and Party put away;
  Here, hand in hand, we proudly say—
"We're first Canadians and men."

J. W. BENGOUGH.

LEADER-WRITING.

A LONDON editor told me that he had lost his leader-writer. I said that I supposed he would easily get another. "I shall have to get three," was his reply; "and I shall be lucky if at the end of a year one of them writes well." He meant, of course, not that leader-writing was a work of uncommon genius, but that the knack was rare.

There seem to be three requisites: a large amount of information, miscellaneous rather than profound; a great readiness in making use of it; and the power of putting it in a striking form, and one which will catch the eye and mind of the cursory reader. As to the first, it was once proposed to create a college for journalists, treating journalism as a regular profession, and teaching all the subjects likely to be required. But I always doubted the feasibility of such a scheme. The matter is too indefinite, and journalism is too little of a regular profession.

The second requisite is evidently a gift of nature. A man must be blest with great natural quickness if, when he is sitting at a dinner party, and a note from his editor with a subject is suddenly put into his hand, he can jump up and have a good article ready for press. Form perhaps comes to few writers by nature, but may be acquired by study of good models. John Douglas Cook, the editor of the *Saturday Review*, an excellent judge of writing, though he could not write himself, told me that the only writers within his experience, which was large, who wrote well from the first, had been trained at school in the composition of Latin verse. This may have been not wholly accidental. Cook's experience must have had reference to papers other than the *Saturday Review*, the articles in which, the paper being social rather than political, and non-partisan, were essays rather than leaders.

Good leader-writing is certainly rarer than one would suppose, and when I was in London fetched a high price. The greatest sensation that I remember ever being produced by a leader was one written by Bailey in the *Times* when Peel came over from Protection to Free Trade. But then the subject was most momentous, and the *Times* had early intelligence.

The position of a leader-writer in England must have changed with the character of the press. In former days the proprietor and editor of a great paper, such as the *Times* or the Leeds *Mercury*, was a sort of literary statesman guiding his paper according to his own opinions, though in concert with his political party. Now journalism seems to have become more entirely commercial, aiming above everything at circulation, largely by sensational means. This can hardly be congenial to a serious writer.

At a time when, after the fall of Peel's Government,

parties in England were very much broken up and connexions loosened, it was proposed to bring out a paper of news without editorials, but with an open forum for free debate. Gladstone smiled on the idea, but he thought the existing custom of combining comment with news too inveterate to be changed.

It is hardly necessary to mention that the leader belongs, and the responsibility attaches, exclusively to the paper. A friend of mine wanted to reproduce some leaders which he had written in the *Times*, but the *Times* at once vetoed.

GOLDWIN SMITH.

WILLIAM GILLESPY
Founder and First President of the Canadian Press Association

THE CANADIAN PRESS ASSOCIATION

I.

A PERIOD OF TURMOIL

THE Canadian Press Association, which holds its fiftieth annual meeting in 1908, was organized at Kingston in the month of September, 1859. It came into existence, after many efforts, in a modest way. There were, at that period, exceptional obstacles to overcome before even a semblance of union and harmony could be established among the newspapers of Canada. The founders of the Association were well aware of the adverse conditions to be encountered, and only the virtues of patience, courage, and enthusiasm could have carried the movement to success.

At the outset it is proper to make clear the difficulties which stood in the way of a general press organization. The Canada of 1859, nominally one Province with a united Parliament and all the outward aspect of solidarity, really consisted of two separate communities, each having its own history, language, and ideas. There was political and social disunion. The influences tending towards strife and estrangement were all-powerful. The ties that commonly bind communities

1

together were weak, and party dissensions invaded the domain of the press, with consequences disastrous to personal friendship and to the tone of discussion. To aggravate the situation still further some of our chief public men were themselves journalists. As Principal Grant said of the rise of Joseph Howe in Nova Scotia, "at that time in the history of the world it was almost impossible to be an editor without being a politician also." * This had long been an embarrassing factor in the connection between politics and the press. The rebellion in Upper Canada was promoted and led by an editor. The Quebec journalists were equally prominent in the movement there. As time wore on the issues of the day involved principles of prime importance to the State, and it was natural that writers for the press should be leading figures in the fray. These issues touched the very core of national life. A conflict that questioned the loyalty of the citizen to the State easily glided into attacks on personal character. The ten years that preceded the formation of the Press Association are pre-eminent for the bitterness that prevailed between parties, or sections of parties, and between individuals. In this atmosphere editors vied with politicians in vehemence of tone and wealth of expletive. Francis Hincks, who founded the Toronto *Examiner* in 1838, and the Montreal *Pilot* in 1844, never to the end of his long and varied career quite abandoned journalistic pursuits. His course in 1854, when he, the Prime Minister and nominal leader of the Reform party, passed over the Government of the country to a Conservative Coalition—a modified

* Joseph Howe ; by Rev. G. M. Grant; Halifax, 1906.

form of "dishing the Whigs"—intensified the bitterness of feeling. The resentment of George Brown and *The Globe* at the fate of the Short Administration and the aspect of deep duplicity given to it by the Double Shuffle was at its height in 1859. D'Arcy McGee in the Montreal *New Era* displayed Celtic effervescence in all its purity. William McDougall, never famous for conciliatory methods in press or Parliament, was writing his telling articles in the *North American.* Each party was split into warring factions. Neither was a happy family. The progressive wing of the Tory party, led by John A. Macdonald, was in open revolt against the remnant of the FamilyCompact under Sir Allan McNab and HillyardCameron. TheReformers, weakened by the defection of the Hincksites, were at loggerheads with *le parti Rouge* from Lower Canada. George Brown, as we read in Mr. Mackenzie's biography of him, decided to retire from public life. John A. Macdonald, early in 1859, made the same resolution. A signed requisition from his Parliamentary following alone kept him in the field. The honest zeal of men for their own opinions had gone too far. The spirit of moderate compromise necessary to support any political fabric seemed to be vanishing altogether.

It was at this critical juncture that the founders of the Press Association made their appeal to the sober counsels and kindly feelings that were in danger of being extinguished. Their task was no easy one. The press, unlike the medical and legal professions, does not readily lend itself to organization. The community of interest in the journalistic fraternity is of delicate texture. The tie between the editor and his readers is closer than the bond between editors as a class. Those were not the days of great publishing concerns with important financial concerns in common. A Press Association could hold out no tempting material advantages to its members. The Association, never an insurance society, offered little to individual selfishness. The appeal was chiefly to the highest form of professional pride—to promote the influence of the press as a factor in the welfare of the State, to draw closer together as a body when the tendencies of the time were pointing to national disintegration. The leading spirit in the movement for union was William Gillespy of the Hamilton *Spectator*. Previous to the Kingston meeting, there must have been an interchange of views by correspondence between a number of newspaper editors upon the propriety of organization, because the *Spectator* of September 24th refers in a cheerful strain to 1859 as a kind of *annus mirabilis*, when Blondin was able to walk over the Niagara chasm on a tight-rope; a balloon had just made a journey one thousand miles long; and fifty or sixty Canadian journalists had expressed their willingness "to throw aside their political differences for the nonce in order that they may commune together for the purpose of mutually benefitting each other in matters pertaining to the general welfare of the Fourth Estate."

In that year the Provincial Exhibition was being held in Kingston. This was considered to be a suitable time for the gathering, because the event would draw together a number of newspaper representatives, not specially concerned at the moment to determine whether or not Hincks was a traitor, George Brown a bigot, or John A. Macdonald a thoroughly used-up character. The more peaceful occupation of inspecting cattle, grain, fruit, and flowers would, it was thought, give at least a temporary impetus to those humane instincts which, on too many other occasions, were allowed to remain dormant.

II.

FOUNDING OF THE ASSOCIATION.

As everyone who has tried to hold meetings of newspaper men is aware, the labours of Hercules were trifles in comparison. The journalistic mind is so constituted that it recoils instinctively from long speeches, aimless resolutions, and conventional proceedings. Nearly every newspaper writer has, at some period in his career, been a reporter. This means that he has often suffered from the public bore, and is unwilling to revive, even for the benefit of his own fraternity, the wearisome paraphernalia that cluster about the formation of new societies. The Kingston gathering challenged this prejudice. Of the fifty or sixty persons who had written their approval of the projected Association, few were found ready to leave their work, travel long distances, and formally participate in the act of organization. The earnestness of those who made the necessary sacrifices, however, was irresistible. Having conquered the deep-seated opposition inherent in the political conditions of the time, they were not to be daunted by that degree of apathy expressed in mere bodily absence. The first meeting, called for the afternoon of September 27th, was adjourned in order to secure a larger attendance. The following evening a sufficient number of newspaper men came together and the project took shape. The list of those present is interesting:

William Gillespy, Hamilton *Spectator*.
Dr. Barker, Kingston *Whig*.
Mackenzie Bowell, Belleville *Intelligencer*.
David Wylie, Brockville *Recorder*.
J. E. P. Doyle, Cornwall *Freeholder*.
Thomas Sellar, Montreal *Echo*.
John Jacques, Milton *Journal*.
R. J. Oliver, Barrie *Advance*.
John Lowe, Montreal *Gazette*.
Dr. Gillespie, Picton *Times*.
Dunbar Browne, Montreal *Gazette*.
W. A. Sheppard, Belleville *Independent*.
W. Armstrong, Kingston *Herald*.
J. Beach, Whitby *Watchman*.
Mr. Campbell, Napanee *Standard*.
W. G. Culloden, Milton *New Era*.
James Somerville, Dundas *Banner*.
H. C. Grant, Kingston *News*.

Mr. Gillespy was called to the chair. It is asserted by all who know the early history of the Association that Mr. Gillespy was the life and soul of the movement. His must have been a frank and generous nature to secure the co-operation of confreres who differed from him in politics at a time when all men seemed to take their politics very seriously. Of English birth—his native city being Carlisle—he emigrated to Canada in 1842, at the age of 18, and soon after is known as a writer for the Conservative press. To that party he always adhered, nor is it charged that he held

his opinions lightly.   Decided in his views, he possessed
a genial and kindly temperament which well fitted
the part he was to play.   Displaying some literary
talent in a volume of verse and some short tales, he
ultimately found his vocation as a political writer
about the time Lord Metcalfe was disputing with his
Ministers over the question of responsible government.
Connected for short periods with the Brantford *Courier*
and London (U.C.) *Times*, he entered, in 1850, the
office of the Hamilton *Spectator* as bookkeeper.   It is
noteworthy that the division between the counting
room and the editorial office was not then so clearly
defined as it is now commonly, although often erroneously, held to be.   In due course he became the sole
proprietor and editor of the paper, and was, therefore,
an influential figure at the Kingston gathering.   To
David Wylie fell the honour of moving a resolution in
favor of organizing an Association, and the motion
was carried unanimously.   A committee to draft a
constitution was named, consisting of Messrs Gillespy,
Barker, Wylie, and Oliver, and the members adjourned
to meet later in Toronto and elect officers.

The new Association commanded the support of a
considerable number of journalists in Upper Canada.*

---

* In the Canadian Newspaper Directory for 1858, published in Toronto by
W. Meikle, the names of all the journals issued in Canada at that date are
given. There were 20 dailies, 18 tri-weeklies, 15 semi-weeklies, and 156
weeklies. In classifying them politically, Mr. Meikle unconsciously reveals
the state of public opinion, for he divides them into Protestants and Roman
Catholics. Of 43 Conservative papers, three, he says, "may more
appropriately be termed Tory." There were 47 Reform journals, all stoutly
Protestant, while of the 57 Liberal or independent a large proportion (sad to
relate) supported "a sort of demi-Roman Catholic principle." Two journals
successfully dodged Mr. Meikle's creed test and he mournfully puts them
down as neutral in politics and religion.

Its early years were years of struggle and difficulty from causes already mentioned. The first meetings were not well attended. In Toronto some of the chief men held aloof. In Lower Canada it took no hold even among the writers for the English press. This, perhaps, was natural, because in those days long distances could not be overcome in a few hours by a rapid and comfortable railway journey. If the political connection between Montreal and Toronto was closer, by reason of Parliament meeting in Quebec, than it is now, the intercourse of the members of the newspaper fraternity was not constant. But the founders and first members of the Association were a loyal band. They were attached to the Association and to the friendships formed there. Some of them rose to great prominence in the life of the country. Forty years afterwards one of them, Sir Mackenzie Bowell, who had advanced to the post of Prime Minister of Canada, said in addressing the Ottawa meeting of the Association:

"When I look back at the number of years that have passed since I assisted Mr. Gillespy, then editor of the Hamilton *Spectator*, in forming this Association, I am beginning to think I am a tolerably old man. However that may be, I can assure you that my heart is still with you—just as strongly as it was before I entered that political world, outside of that which pertains to newspaper writers. It has always been a matter of congratulation to me to see the unanimity which exists among the newspaper men of the country. And I always remember with pleasure that I was of some assistance in forming, in the earlier period of my life, an Association in which I have formed friendships—with many with whom I am not in political accord—which have never ceased to exist to the present day."

That the principal aim of the new body was to promote friendly feelings and social intercourse amongst its members is undoubted. In the records which have fortunately survived from the past there is a brief sketch of the Association from the pen of its first President. "The design of forming themselves into an Association," he declares, "had long engaged the attention of, and been discussed by, the editorial fraternity of Canada. But not so much with the object of self-protection, as a means of bringing together at stated times the members of the Fourth Estate, and thus affording them opportunities of becoming better acquainted with one another. It was thought, and rightly so too, as experience has proved, that annual re-unions would tend to smooth down the asperities which are apt to spring up, and check, if not entirely remove in a short time, the bitterness of tone the press had unfortunately assumed; and it was finally decided to attempt an organization of some kind."

III.

THE FIRST LIST OF OFFICERS.

EARLY in February, 1860, the adjourned meeting was held in the Mechanics' Institute, Toronto, and officers were elected as follows:

President: Wm. Gillespy, Hamilton *Spectator*.

First Vice-President: Gordon Brown, Toronto *Globe*.

Second Vice-President: Josiah Blackburn, London *Free Press*.

Hon. Sec.: D. McDougall, Berlin *Telegraph*.

Sec.-Treas.: Thomas Sellar, Montreal *Echo*.

Executive Committee: George Sheppard, Toronto *Globe;*

James Seymour, St. Catharines *Constitutional;*

James Somerville, Dundas *Banner;*

Thomas McIntosh, Brantford *Expositor;*

John Jacques, Milton *Journal*.

Of these the only survivors, so far as the writer knows, are Mr. Somerville and Mr. Sheppard. Mr. Somerville, who represented the riding of North Brant in the Canadian Parliament for many years, is a good type of the men who founded the Association and became a strong influence in promoting the welfare and standing of the press. He had established the Dundas *Banner* in 1858, and was a young man of 25 when he joined Gillespy and the others in organizing the Association. He lived to fill every municipal office, being mayor of Dundas, his native town, and warden of the County of Wentworth, finally going to the House of Commons as the crowning stage in a career of usefulness and honour. Mr. Sheppard, during his connection with the Canadian press, displayed remarkable gifts. He was born in England, and being in early life apprenticed to a bookseller and printer, cultivated literary talents of no mean order. The reading of Godwin's "Political Justice" created a marked impression on his mind, and led to his forming strong views on political questions. He became a contributor to Radical papers, chiefly in the North of England, and addressed meetings on educational and labour topics. Coming to Canada, after more than one visit to the United States, he was at first an actuary for the Canada Life Assurance Company in Hamilton. But his tastes naturally drew him back to journalism. It was he who penned the famous article in the *Colonist*, "Whither are we Drifting?" and caused a sensation of the first magnitude. Having thus broken with the Conservatives, he joined *The Globe* and was a prominent figure in the great Reform Convention at Toronto in 1859. He afterwards served on the Quebec press and retired to live in the United States. He now resides near Boston. Not long ago he visited Toronto, and among the few surviving friends whom he found to call upon was Mr. H. P. Dwight of the Great North-Western Telegraph Company, a vigorous veteran of the Fifties like himself. Mr. Somerville was an active member of the Association during many years and was its President in 1871. Mr. Sheppard, however, was not long enough in Canada to attend the meetings. Nor did Mr. Gordon Brown connect himself with the work of the Association, although he was always held in high esteem by its members, and even after leaving journalism for a post in the Ontario Civil Service, he continued to take a keen interest in all that pertained to the press. That his pen, rather than that of his famous brother, gave to *The Globe* its character for vigorous writing and profound grasp of political issues is generally believed. Mr. Dent in "The Last Forty Years" pays this tribute to the qualities of Gordon Brown:

"Mr. John Gordon Brown, though he has never entered Parliamentary life, is almost as widely known in the Dominion as his elder brother. His very exceptional journalistic ability has been displayed upon *The Globe* for more than thirty years, and has materially contributed to maintain that journal in the high rank which it achieved at an early period of its career."

Another of the first office-bearers was Mr. Sellar, who so loyally assisted Mr. Gillespy in tiding the Association over the initial period of apathy. Mr. Sellar came to Canada in 1852 from Scotland, where he was born at Elgin in 1828. Entering the counting room of *The Globe*, he was for a long time, it is recorded, the only clerk needed in the office. Mr. George Brown advised him to try a country paper. Thus in 1857 he acquired the Brampton *Times*, which he sold to Mr. Tye shortly after, returning to Toronto as publisher of the *Echo*, a Church of England organ. Subsequently removing the paper to Montreal, he continued to publish it until his death in 1867. Mr. Sellar was elected President of

the Association at its Montreal meeting in 1866, and
journeyed to distant Goderich in August, 1867, when
the dawn of the new Dominion was referred to in patriotic terms in the presidential address His lamented
death occurred shortly after. His successor in office,
Mr. J. A. Campbell, at the Collingwood meeting in the
following year, made a feeling reference to the services
rendered by Mr. Sellar:

"The extra and untiring exertion used to establish
the Association by our late President is well known
to many of you, and while we mourn his loss and the
absence of his lively encouragement to press forward
in our good undertaking, we cannot but rejoice at
the result of his energy and zeal, when we see the
present large and respectable union of editors holding different political views and met for a common
cause."

The Association, having elected officers and adopted
a constitution, was now fairly launched. The constitution, like the short and simple annals of the poor,
might raise a disdainful smile amongst pretentious
persons. But it was practical and adequate for all
purposes and forms the basis of the present constitution.
There is a faded little book among the surviving records
which must have been the Association's first ledger.
The initial entry bears date February 8th, 1860, and
the treasurer closed his year triumphantly with a sur-
plus of $21.79. The annual subscription was one
dollar, and the money raised paid the expenses of
the meetings. The society was not rich, but many
of the charges were doubtless defrayed out of the
members' own pockets, and the cost of the handsome

silver service presented to Mr. Gillespy on his retirement from the presidency was paid by special subscription.

Mr. Gillespy was President for three years, when he insisted on vacating the office, which was filled by Mr. McDougall. Twice the annual meeting was held in Hamilton, where the founder gave proofs of his hospitable and genial disposition. Writing some of his recollections for the Kingston *Whig* years afterwards, Mr. Gillespy said:

"It is well nigh a quarter of a century since the efforts to place the newspaper press of this country upon a higher level were crowned with success—a movement which few can deny has done much to elevate its tone, while it united and harmonized, by social intercourse, many who had long been estranged. I rejoice that I had an active part in the work, and that I have lived to see the good effected through the instrumentality of such a happy combination of the brethren of the press. It makes me sad when I think of the career in which I found so much enjoyment, and in the company of a noble band of men, so many of whom have gone to their account. What a noble galaxy there were! George Brown, Hugh Scobie, Robert R. Smiley, Thomas McQueen, John Sheridan Hogan, Daniel Morrison, James Moir Ferres, Marcus Talbot, Thomas Sellar, Samuel Amsden, W. J. Cox, H. C. Grant, J. S. Gurnett, John Jacques, Thomas Messenger, and many more whom I cannot name. Then, happily, there are still in the land of the living Dr. Barker, David Wylie, Mackenzie Bowell, Caldwell, Young, Somerville, Siddons, Jackson, Buckingham, Cameron, Blackburn, McDougall, and a host of others, all of whom were active in the work of bringing the press to its present enviable position."

This was in 1883, and now, another quarter of a century later, we have fortunately still with us Mr. Buckingham, Sir Mackenzie Bowell, Mr. Cameron, Mr. Young, and Mr. Somerville.

The Hamilton meeting of 1860, held in September, was simultaneous with the visit of the Prince of Wales (the present King) to that city, and the functions connected with Royalty naturally overshadowed the quiet celebration of the young Association. A public breakfast was given at the Anglo-American Hotel, and Mr. C. J. Brydges, the well-known railway manager, was the guest of the members.

In 1861 the meeting was held in London, when, at the public dinner, the guests of the Association included Thomas D'Arcy McGee, Hon. M. H. Foley, the Postmaster-General, and Mayor Bowes, of Toronto. Mr. Foley's connection with the press had ceased some years before, but he retained his friendly relations with the fraternity and lent a sympathetic ear to the representations made to him in his official capacity respecting the iniquities of the postal law. This law, as we shall presently see, was always the *bête noir* of the Association. Mr. Foley came to Canada with his parents from Ireland. Having taught school for a time, he began to study law, and for nearly ten years edited several Reform journals, including the Simcoe *Messenger*.

Mr. McGee, whose remarkable talents had not as yet landed him in office, but whose ardent disposition

HON. SIR MACKENZIE BOWELL, K.C.M.G.
President 1865 and a Charter Member

readily adapted itself to the journalistic controversies of the day, seems to have been impressed favourably by the purposes and aims of the Press Association. Years afterwards, when addressing a Montreal audience in the Confederation year, his memory reverted to the occasion at London, and he spoke eloquently of the functions which the press could discharge in the development of the new Dominion. "I may observe," he said, "that there is a Press Association—hitherto flourishing chiefly in Ontario—which it may be hoped will be extended to the whole Dominion. In this Association the public are more interested than they are aware of. It is a first attempt, long required, to extend the laws of personal courtesy and good faith to this all-powerful fraternity. If it succeeds it will be no longer possible for a man to utter behind a printing press what he dare not take the personal responsibility of stating in a private room, or anywhere else. If it succeeds it abridges the privileges of scoundrelism; but it elevates the reputation of the whole class. It will go far in placing the editor on the same professional plane with the Faculty and the Bar, and, by enforcing on their profession their own laws, will obviate the intervention of the civil power, always to be regretted, even when rendered unavoidable in relation to the Press."

2

IV.

METHODS AND MEN OF EARLY DAYS.

ATTENDANCE at the annual meetings in the early Sixties was a far severer test of attachment to the Association than any that is set the members to-day. Not only were railways fewer, and the custom of going to conventions less firmly established, but the editor was a busier person. The newspaper office, at that period, demanded the services of that important personage the "all-round man." There was thorough training of a practical sort for both hand and brain. Perhaps in no single respect has the past been more completely revolutionized than in the management and production of newspapers. "Down to the time of the founders of the Canadian Press Association," says Mr. William Buckingham, "no change had been made in the system of Gutenberg, the inventor of movable types. The letters, as cast in the foundry, continued to be picked up by hand singly from their several boxes in the case and were formed into lines in the composing stick—so different from the process that has developed under our own eyes, of setting together the matrices by highly complex machines and casting from them solid metallic lines. But although the old manner of preparing matter for the press was centuries

behind present-day methods in the mechanical art
of type-setting, it trained in the humaner sort of literary composition a progressive class of men. The printing office was a school, enabling many a boy without
early advantages to rise to good positions in the newspaper profession and in the service of the State. As he
set type he educated himself, acquired literary tastes,
became in turn local and parliamentary reporter,
writer of descriptive and leading articles, editor and
proprietor of a newspaper of his own. Looking over
the lists of the men who were members of this Association in the early days of its history, one is struck by the
number who made for themselves careers from these
humble beginnings. Some of these men are with us
yet, but they are becoming fewer all the time, for the
newspaper field is no longer the recruiting ground of
former days. Graduation, the chance to rise step by
step, has gone. The blend of printer, news-gatherer,
reporter, editor, has disappeared, and each man begins,
continues, and ends in his own particular niche." This
accurately depicts the older school of journalism.

"At first," says Mr. John Cameron, "a large major-
ity of the Association were proprietors, editors, and
all-round men. On the whole, the reporting on the
best country papers forty years ago was better than
most of present-day reporting. It was all-round reporting: in the case of a meeting, for example, giving
more of colour and atmosphere than is often noticed
in modern reporting. Then, the papers depended
more, relatively, on subscriptions, and less, relatively,
on advertisements. The advertising end of a newspaper did not then dominate to the injurious extent

that it does to-day. To-day, in news, 'sporting' is
the principal feature, the space given up to 'sport'
being proportionately ten-fold greater than even a
quarter of a century ago. This excessive catering to
'sport' cannot be considered an advantage or improvement."

The work then, on the whole, was more attractive
than ours. It produced men of strong personal
quality, because it gave free vent to the individual.
Mr. Gillespy left on record a graphic sketch of the
pioneers and their work. "There was William Lyon
Mackenzie, misguided man that he was," wrote the
genial old Conservative editor, "yet probably the most
industrious who ever wielded a pen. I have seen him
sitting at his Parliamentary desk, in his stocking feet,
the busiest man in the House, with paste pot and
scissors before him, poring over 'exchanges,' or trans-
ferring cuttings from them ready to be commented
upon in his paper, the *Message*, as soon as he found
leisure. There were other newspaper writers who did
work for their journals in Parliament, but none of
them worked like Mr. Mackenzie.

"When George Brown and his father guided the
destinies of *The Globe*, Dr. Ryerson was writing his
'defence' of Sir Charles Metcalfe for the *British Colonist* while the *Patriot* was thundering against the Cabinet Ministers with whom Sir Charles had quarreled.
Party spirit ran high and the Press and Parliament
vied in bitterness and the determination to win in the
battle of party strife. Toronto had not, however, a
monopoly of newspaper warfare very long; a like spirit
had imbued others who soon found themselves in the

midst of the fray. Outside the Provincial Capital there were journals just as able as they were willing to go into the fight; and they did so. The Long Point *Advocate* was one of the foremost, the editor being Mr. Foley. Many a flaying he administered to luckless wights, and many another he received, his principal antagonist being Mr. Smiley. He abandoned journalism and became a legislator; and as a disappointed man, at a Ministerial banquet, dubbed the Cabinet he supported as 'Scotch and all Scotch.' This disclosed his want of fealty to his party, and he afterwards joined the opposite side. Mr. Foley's true element was in a newspaper office.

"Robert Spence, who became Postmaster-General by a sudden turn of the political wheel, was a newspaper man, and wrote valiantly as a Reformer, but gave up his journal, the Dundas *Warder*, on becoming a Cabinet Minister. John Sheridan Hogan was a sort of free lance on the press. He won the prize for the best essay on Canada at the great French Exhibition, was a contributor to *Blackwood*, Parliamentary correspondent, and lastly publisher and editor of the *United Empire*. He was unhappy, ill-starred, peevish, and inclined always to take the gloomiest view of everything. A long and intimate acquaintance with him gave me an insight into his real character, and to use one of his own favourite expressions, 'I do say,' that in spite of himself Hogan was a good fellow at heart. Like Marcus Talbot, he came to an untimely end. This brings me to speak of the last named; he also was a journalist. Freeman Talbot, in order to lash the Government for dismissing him from office, started the *Prototype* in London, but soon got tired of it and sold out to Marcus, who, after winning his way into Parliament, was lost in the steamship Hungarian on returning from his wedding trip to Europe.

"Canadian newspaperdom gradually extended its area, as the facilities for starting new journals increased. In a short time nearly every town of the least importance had its newspaper, and now many of them have more than one. The press has grown into a mighty power in this fair Dominion, and will compare favorably with that of the country alongside of us. Men of letters, means, and spirit embarked in the enterprise, and now, after some of the older heads have been laid low, and others are yet calmly surveying the wonderful change that has 'come over the spirit of their dreams,' the work goes deftly on at an accelerated pace. Young men of ability found it to their advantage to join a profession that had hitherto been regarded as the sole field for the exercise of the talents of a few, and to-day it is the proud boast of our country that most of its journals are in able and worthy hands."

V.

SOME PIONEERS OF THE ASSOCIATION.

In the views just quoted, which Mr. Gillespy wrote for the Kingston *Whig* in 1884, are reflected the sentiments of the men who founded the Association. They were proud of their profession. Not blind to its defects, they admired the talents of all who contributed to make the press influential. In them there was the true spirit of *camaraderie*. The first President proclaimed his belief without hesitation. He had able coadjutors. There was David Wylie of Brockville, who filled the editorial chair of the *Recorder* for many years, and who rarely missed a meeting of the Association.* One finds him at Hamilton, at Toronto, at Goderich, at Kingston, until, attaining a green old age, he was hailed as the "father of the press." The active membership in early days included those who were termed "ex-publishers," so that the younger fry were stimulated by the presence of the veterans. It is well, therefore, to recall their services and to leave on record the kind of men they were. Mr. Wylie, by birth a Scotchman, was trained to the printing business. He was a reporter at one time for the Liverpool *Mail* and came to Canada

* The compiler of this record is indebted for much biographical material to three valuable works by Dr. Henry J. Morgan of Ottawa, namely, Celebrated Canadians, 1862; Bibliotheca Canadensis, 1867; Canadian Men and Women of the Time, 1898.

in 1845. He acted as Parliamentary reporter for the
Montreal *Herald*, and then bought, in 1849, the Brockville *Recorder*, in the columns of which he upheld for
many years the policy of the Liberal party. Mr.
Wylie wrote well both in prose and verse and was never
more at home than in a group of newspaper men.

Thomas White was from the first another staunch
member. In after time when he had become a public
man, in the front rank of his party, he was still with affec-
tionate familiarity hailed as "Tom." He and his brother
Richard White—still the honoured chief of the Montreal
Gazette—had established in 1853 the Peterborough
Review, a weekly journal expressing at first the views
of the Baldwin Reformers, but soon afterwards casting
in its lot with the party of Sir John Macdonald. One
brother devoted himself to the business management,
while the other controlled the editorial policy. In
1865 the Hamilton *Spectator* was purchased by the
White brothers from Mr. Gillespy, and in July, 1870,
they bought the Montreal *Gazette*. Political life soon
cast its spell over Thomas White. He was an unsuc-
cessful candidate in South Wentworth for the Ontario
Legislature in 1867, but turned his attention later to
Parliament and was elected for Cardwell in 1878. As
a Parliamentarian his gifts were universally recognized,
and, in 1885, he was appointed Minister of the Interior in
the Macdonald Government, at that time a most ardu-
ous post owing to the Riel Rebellion. To his public
duties he gave his best energies, and his unexpected
death in 1888, after a short illness, deprived Canada of
an able and valiant son. He retained a warm regard
for the press years after he had handed over the manag-

ing editorship of the *Gazette* to his son, Robert S. White. On his appointment to the Privy Council, he was given a banquet by the Montreal press, irrespective of party. In 1883 Mr. White delivered in Montreal a valuable lecture on Canadian newspapers. It contained much interesting historical data which he had industriously collected from various sources not then as accessible to the student as they are now. Mr. White reminded his hearers of the strides made by the Canadian newspapers in providing promptly the news of the day by telegraph. "On one occasion," he said, "a budget night in Parliament, one Montreal morning paper contained nineteen columns of matter, every line of which was written in Ottawa after five o'clock of the previous afternoon, telegraphed to Montreal, re-written in the telegraph office here, set up in type, the proofs read and corrected, the paper printed, the early mails served, and the delivery to subscribers in the city accomplished so that the matter could be read at the early breakfast table." Thus had the journalist of the older school responded effectively to the exacting demands of the modern daily press. Mr. White was President of the Association at the Brockville meeting in 1865.

Another pioneer of note is Honourable James Young, of Galt, still happily in the land of the living. Purchasing the Dumfries *Reformer* in 1853, Mr. Young gave ten years of efficient writing and vigorous thinking to the Liberal cause. Entering Parliament in 1867, he continued to display the intelligent and independent qualities which made him a man of mark on the press. He wrote treatises on the Reciprocity Treaty and the Agricultural Resources of Canada, both of which won prizes in public competition, and were the fruits of a well-stored mind. Severing active connection with the press in 1863, Mr. Young is not so prominent in the later proceedings of the Association as some others, but he gives in his book "Public Men and Public Life in Canada," a pleasant chronicle of the meeting in 1862.

In the pages of the quaint little ledger of the Association, beginning with the entries of 1860, one sees the names of others who became famous in journalistic or Parliamentary history. One of these is Rufus Stephenson, editor and publisher of the Chatham *Planet*, and for a long period member of the House of Commons for the County of Kent. Mr. Stephenson passed his youth at St. Catharines, where his family had settled. Well versed in all branches of the printing art, he began writing for the Chatham *Advertiser*, and in 1850 joined the staff of the *Planet* as associate editor. In a few years he became proprietor and editor of the paper, and before Confederation was a prominent advocate of the Conservative policy, exhibiting, as is recorded in a biographical sketch of that date, "very considerable talent and power as a political writer." In the educational and municipal interests of Chatham he was long a leading figure, being Mayor of the town for several years. A strong supporter of the Union, he was returned to Parliament in 1867. He represented Kent during four Parliaments, survived the Conservative Waterloo in 1874, and was one of Sir John Macdonald's "Old Guard." He was appointed Collector of Customs for Chatham, and died in that official position in 1901.

Yet another familiar name is that of Mr. William

Buckingham, now of Stratford, whose newspaper career is full of interest and variety. Born in England, where for four years he was on the staff of the Halifax *Guardian*, Mr. Buckingham emigrated to this country, and was connected until 1859 with the Toronto *Globe*. The story of how he and his friend William Coldwell, a reporter on the Toronto *Leader* staff, began the publication of the *Nor'Wester* at Fort Garry in that year is one of romantic adventure. It has been graphically related by Mr. E. B. Biggar. The two friends journeyed to the far distant Red River settlement by way of Minnesota. They bought a hand press in Toronto and their printing supplies in St. Paul. Then they started across the prairie by ox-cart. The oxen were wild as March hares, and the cart with the type galloped wildly along the way until it upset and the pioneers had a lively experience with pi. The journey was long and laborious. They passed through swamps and over stumps of trees and up and down hills. "Red Lake River," wrote Mr. Coldwell to a friend in Toronto, "the wildest, deepest, crookedest, and swiftest, took some of us up to our necks and nearly took me out of this vale of tears altogether." Mr. Coldwell had taken his silk hat with him, and as the easiest way of carrying it, had worn it on his head. To see him up to his neck in Red River with a silk hat bobbing above the surface must have been a funny sight. After sleeping in tents and dodging Indians and wolves, the party reached their destination, and the first number of the fortnightly *Nor'Wester* was issued at Fort Garry on December 28th, 1859. Soon after, William Lyon Mackenzie wrote in his *Message:* "I was once the most western editor, bookseller, and printer in British America, but the *Nor'Wester* is a thousand miles beyond me." This explains why the name of William Buckingham of the Stratford *Beacon* does not appear in the Association's ledger until September 6th, 1865. Having sold his interests in the West, he returned to Canada, edited the Simcoe *Reformer* for a time, and in 1863 acquired the *Beacon*. His career since is what might be expected from talent and force of character. He was official reporter of the London conference on the Confederation Bill in 1866, private secretary to the Honourable Alexander Mackenzie during the latter's Premiership, and was appointed Deputy Minister of the Interior in 1878. By an act of partizanship, not defensible in any Government, he was deprived of that office by the Conservatives. In municipal, commercial, and benevolent work, he has been a foremost citizen of Stratford. To him, associated with Honourable G. W. Ross, we owe the biography of the great Liberal Premier.

One is tempted to linger over the names of these pioneer members. There is John Maclean, the father of several newspaper editors (W. F. Maclean, M.P., being one), who expounded the protectionist doctrine so ably when others hung back, and whose *Illustrated News*, published at Hamilton in the Sixties, is the first of our pictorial weeklies; John Cameron, who, as the valiant champion of Liberalism in the *Advertiser*, was called to the management of the Toronto *Globe* and is now postmaster of London; W. R. Climie, who joined in 1863 and served for fourteen years as secretary; J. W. Carman, of the old Kingston *British American*, a stalwart in the Liberal journalism of

Eastern Ontario; Erastus Jackson, of the Newmarket *Era*, who was secretary for three years, President in 1870, and is yet in the ranks of hardy veterans; James Innes, esteemed by all, who sat in Parliament for South Wellington, and made the Guelph *Mercury* a power; J. S. Larke, of the Oshawa *Vindicator*, now Canada's representative in Australia; and Alexander McLean, of the Cornwall *Freeholder*, acting in a similar capacity in Japan; James Shannon of the Kingston *News*, afterwards postmaster of Kingston; Josiah Blackburn, an accomplished writer, and a chief ornament of Western Ontario journalism; James Seymour, of the St. Catharines *Constitutional*, a writer and publisher of renown for twenty years, and for nearly another twenty a useful official in the Inland Revenue service.

All these, and many more, were on the Association's rolls before Confederation. It is impossible to name them all. But it is due to history before leaving this goodly list to relate the story of a certain witty telegram to Sir John Macdonald, which will survive when all of us have passed to where beyond these voices there is peace. It has been erroneously attributed to Mr. Blackburn, but really emanated from Mr. Robert Smiley, of Hamilton. The *Spectator* in 1854 was attacking Hon. Robert Spence, who sat for North Wentworth as a Reformer. When the Coalition was formed, Spence became a colleague of John A. Macdonald, who promptly pleaded with Smiley to cease firing at a man who would next day be his associate, and Mr. Smiley wired back: "It's a damned sharp curve, but I think we can take it." And he took it, thereby contributing vastly to the gaiety of nations.

VI.

A FAMOUS HAMILTON CONVENTION.

TORONTO was selected as the meeting place for 1862. There were not many present on the date fixed—September 23rd—but those who put in an appearance decided to utilize the occasion to make an appeal to the Government on the postage question. The deputation met the Postmaster-General in the Rossin House. Mr. Foley received the members of his old profession with cordiality. He declared himself in favour of abolishing postage on newspapers and would recommend his colleagues to repeal the law. The revenue was only the richer for the tax by a few thousand dollars, and to cover the loss he would reduce the cost of newspapers purchased for the use of the Department by the amount received from postage. This was the period of short-lived Ministries. Mr. Foley was unable to carry out his policy. But his reply at the time was received, as we are told, "with the liveliest satisfaction by all," and the deputation retired in great good humour. The meeting was not large enough to proceed with further business, so a special session was agreed upon to be held in Hamilton, November 28th. Emboldened by the success of the Toronto deputation, Mr. Gillespy's paper a few days later administered a gentle castigation to the members of the press who had thus far been sceptical of the usefulness of the organization. The *Spectator*, with the vision of free postage before its eyes, remarked:

"We trust that those members of the press who have stood aloof from the Association on the ground that it had accomplished nothing, will now see that they have done injustice to the Association. The value of such an institution is only beginning to be appreciated, it has had the cold shoulder long enough, and the members of the press generally should give its efforts encouragement."

Of the adjourned meeting in Hamilton we have the Hon. James Young's account:* "The first meeting of the Press Association which I attended was held in Hamilton on November 27th of this year. The Association had been formed in Kingston only three years before, and was not then the large and influential body, with an annual banquet, which it is to-day. The following are the names of the principal journalists present on the occasion: Mr. William Gillespy, Hamilton *Spectator;* Mr. Thomas Sellar, of the Montreal *Echo;* Mr. D. McDougall, of the Berlin *Telegraph;* Mr. David Wylie, Brockville *Recorder;* Mr. Thomas White, Jun., Peterboro' *Review;* Mr. Mackenzie Bowell, Belleville *Intelligencer;* Mr. R. E. O'Connor, Ottawa *Union;* Mr. W. G. Culloden, Milton *New Era;* Mr. W. H. Floyd, Cobourg *Star;* Mr. James Young, Galt *Reformer;* Mr. John Jacques, Hamilton *Times;* Mr. George McMullen,

*Public Men and Public Life in Canada: Being Recollections of Parliament and the Press. Toronto, 1902.

Newburg *North American;* Mr. W. T. Cox, Goderich *Huron Signal;* Mr. James A. Campbell, Milton *Champion;* Mr. R. Boyle, Picton *Times;* Mr. John McLean, Sarnia *British Canadian;* Mr. John Siddons, London *Prototype;* Mr. William Mowat, Stratford *Beacon;* Mr. G. W. Verral, Strathroy *Home Guard;* Mr. James Seymour, St. Catharines *Constitutional;* and Mr. W. S. Johnston, Port Hope *Guide.*

"Among the more active members at this meeting of the Press Association were Tom White, as he was then familiarly called, afterwards an honoured member of the Dominion Government; Senator Bowell, still hale and hearty, who has been Premier of Canada and leader of the Conservative party; Mr. D. McDougall, afterwards registrar of the County of Waterloo, and warm-hearted old 'Father Wylie,' as the younger members of the press-gang called him, to his evident pleasure. Those present were a fine body of men, devoted to one of the noblest of professions. But it is also true that in no respect has there been more progress made in Canada since that period than in the growth, the ability, the usefulness and success of our newspaper press. It has been said, 'Those whom the gods love die young.' I know not whether this applies specially to writers for the press, but of those who attended this Hamilton meeting, alas, most of them have already passed over the infinite boundary."

In truth, there is quite a modern air about the Hamilton gathering except that the President positively declined re-election—an archaic sentiment not known in our time. Unlike Julius Cæsar and Oliver Cromwell when offered the crown, Mr. Gillespy really

JOHN A. COOPER
President 1904

ARCH McNEE
President 1905

J. T. CLARK
President 1907-08, and Chairman
of the Semi-Centennial Celebration

J. S. WILLISON
President 1900

meant what he said and was succeeded by Mr. Mc-
Dougall of Berlin. The Association took action respecting postage, of which more anon. The members
also waxed eloquent on the rates charged for quack
medicines. A motion was passed that the foreign rate
should be equal to the local rate, a contention that has
a familiar sound. A committee was appointed to urge
upon the weekly press the wisdom of maintaining a
two dollar subscription rate. This committee is a
remote ancestor of the campaign to force the dailies
above the dollar mark. In the evening there was a
supper, at which Mr. Sellar read a paper on the press
full of curious information about newspapers in ancient
times; Mr. White sang the "Bould Sojer Boy"; and
Mr. Bowell, in a war-like mood, eulogized the volunteers, who would prove an efficient army in case of
invasion. To understand the allusion one should
remember that the Civil War in the States was then
raging, and that the Fenian Raid was casting its bale-
ful shadow ahead with Colonel Bowell on active
service along the banks of the St. Lawrence. In
replying to a toast from the chair: "Success to the
Canadian Press Association," the President-elect
began with the words of an old song:

> Here's to every canty chiel,
> And he that doesna' wish us weel,
> The de'il may rock him in a creel.

Mr. McDougall remarked that it had sometimes been
said that the Association had not accomplished much.
But the objects they aimed at were few. The abolition
of postage they were in a fair way to attain. The other

3

object was to bring the members of the press together in order to do away with those harsh feelings which sometimes characterized their discussions, and the present meeting would have an important bearing on that. The press of Toronto, he said, had endeavored to crush the Association, but the present successful meeting was evidence that it would fail in its endeavors.

VII.

A TRIBUTE TO THE FOUNDER.

BY way of speaking with the enemies in the gate, the next convention was fixed for Toronto in November, 1863. The members who attended were:

D. McDougall, Berlin *Telegraph;* W. Gillespy, Hamilton *Spectator;* Geo. McMullen, Newburg *North American;* G. A. Verral, Strathroy *Home Guard;* G. Miles, Belleville *Chronicle;* H. C. Kennedy, Morrisburg *Courier;* R. Thoroughgood, Simcoe *Reformer;* D. Wylie, Brockville *Recorder;* A. McLachlin, St. Thomas *Journal;* Jas. Seymour, St. Catharines *Constitutional;* Mackenzie Bowell, Belleville *Intelligencer;* Wm. Wallace, Simcoe *British Canadian;* A. G. Belch, St. Mary's *Argus;* J. H. Wood, Kincardine *Review;* Thomas White, Peterborough *Review;* J. A. Campbell, Milton *Champion;* W. T. Cox, Goderich *Signal;* W. R. Climie, Bowmanville *Statesman;* W. H. Floyd, Cobourg *Star;* E. R. Dewhurst, Welland *Telegraph;* W. M. Topping, Galt *Reformer;* H. Cameron, Port Hope *British Canadian;* W. Grant, St. Catharines *Journal;* Thomas Sellar, Montreal *Echo;* W. S. Johnston, Port Hope *Guide;* J. W. Carman, Kingston *British American;* S. L. Roberts, Stratford *Examiner;* John Maclean, Hamilton *Illustrated News.*

No member of the Toronto press was present, and the Association, deeming itself a militant body, complained of the references to the private affairs of editors by two Toronto papers. Adopting the deadly weapon of the Speaker in Parliament, it was decided to "name" the offenders. They were *The Globe* and *The Leader*, and a motion in these terms was passed:

"That in the opinion of this meeting the discussions carried on by journals in Canada, in reference to the personal matters of the proprietors of those journals, are injurious to the character of the press of Canada and are deserving of the censure of this Association."

This bold stroke effected a double purpose. It rebuked the worst sinners and laid down a rule of conduct for the members of the Association themselves. It must not be inferred that Toronto boasted a monopoly of vituperation. In this respect, as in some others, it has lagged behind. The President in his address sorrowfully admitted that "we are all exceedingly prone to violate those acknowledged rules which should govern and regulate our numerous discussions." In fact, as a human being with that liability to error which is characteristic of mere man, Mr. McDougall candidly avowed that there were times of stress when yea, yea, and nay, nay, proved inadequate for the expression of opinions. "It is of course impossible," he said, "in the heat of controversy, which is the natural result of sharp political conflict and keen party warfare, to avoid occasionally stepping beyond the allotted bounds of propriety." However, the protest was needed and produced good effects, even if the two Toronto malefactors continued for some time longer to have strained relations with their reptile contemporaries.

The event of this meeting was the presentation to Mr. Gillespy of a handsome silver tea service and an address which left no doubt of the obligations felt by the members for his staunch effort in the common cause. Mr. Wylie of Brockville, read the address:

TORONTO, *November 12th, 1863.*
To William Gillespy, Esq., Editor and Proprietor of the Hamilton Spectator:

DEAR SIR,—On behalf of the members of the Canadian Press Association, we beg to convey to you the expression of their high appreciation of your services as its leading founder and promoter; and to solicit your acceptance of a tea service as a memento of their regard.

It is well known that to you, more than to any other individual amongst us, the Association is indebted for its origin and progress. You were for the first three years of its existence its chief officer, called to that position by the voice of all the members speaking as one. It has appeared to the members of our Association that we could not part on this occasion of the closing scene of our annual meeting without giving appropriate expression to what we feel, in a manner that will, we trust, make efficient record of the same.

That yourself and your esteemed partner in life may live long and happily, and that we may have the pleasure of meeting you at many more of our annual gatherings, is the heartfelt desire of every member of

our Association, on behalf of which we beg to sub-
scribe ourselves,

Sir, your sincere well wishers,

(Signed) { DAVID WYLIE,
D. McDOUGALL,
M. BOWELL,
THOMAS SELLAR,
THOMAS WHITE.

To which Mr. Gillespy made the following reply:

GENTLEMEN,—You may well imagine how little I
am prepared for this agreeable surprise, for I had no
anticipation of such an episode in the proceedings of
our fourth anniversary. I accept with pleasure your
expression of good will towards me; but permit me to
say that you have greatly overvalued my services to the
Association when you consider them worthy such a
token as you now present me with. That I have
always taken a deep interest in the Press Association
is best shown by the fact that I was its founder, as you
state. I know not, however, that I have done more
than was required of me, and the progress of the
Association is due to more than myself.

Your beautiful present, I assure you, is more than I
deserve, for, having no particular claims upon your
Association, it was not necessary that you should have
singled me out to become the recipient of such a gift.
I accept it, however, as an evidence of your friendship
and esteem, and believe me, it shall be preserved as
a memorial of our institution, for a permanent institution of the country I now regard the Canadian Press
Association.

In behalf of my partner in life, I beg to thank you for your very kind wishes, and at the same time to assure you that she, equally with myself, will appreciate your noble gift. That we may all long be spared to renew our annual gatherings, is the heartfelt prayer of your obliged and humble servant,

WM. GILLESPY.

VIII.

DAWN OF THE EXCURSION PERIOD.

THE Association now entered upon the peripatetic stage of its existence. There was much to be said in behalf of such a policy. The editors personally inspected the attractions of their own country. It enabled them also to become intimate with each other, since there is a proverb that you never really know a man until you have been his fellow-traveller. It ushered in the era of excursions which for a lengthy period were a source of great enjoyment to the members. During the ten years succeeding 1863 one finds the Association at Belleville, Brockville, Montreal, Goderich, Collingwood, Cobourg, Brantford, Toronto, Bracebridge, and London. These were almost entirely summer meetings and an excursion was usually a feature of each of them. Mr. John King, K.C., in former days connected with the Berlin *Telegraph*, and continued in membership later under the rule admitting ex-publishers (and now an honorary member), wrote, in 1876, an agreeable article upon the objects of the Association.* Mr. King thus referred to the advantages conferred by the annual excursion:

"During the first few years of the Association's existence, these holiday trips were of brief duration,

* The Canadian Monthly, June, 1876, p. 532.

and much less pretentious than they have since become. A day and a-half or two days completed the annual meeting and subsequent trip. The whole affair partook more of the character of a large private pleasure party than anything else. But as the Association increased in members, strength, and importance—which it very soon did—the business meeting became more like a miniature congress, and a prolonged holiday more of a felt necessity. The annual excursion has now assumed proportions which make it an event of uncommon public importance. Civic entertainments and *fêtes*, and boundless private hospitalities, attend the Association wherever it goes. The popular notion as to the power and influence of newspapers, as organs of public opinion, has found expression on these occasions in a manner at once complimentary and gratifying. Few cities or towns of any importance where the Association has held its annual gatherings, or which it has visited for any length of time, have not sought to pay it some tribute of public respect, or, in its person, to honour the great and important mission which the Press as a whole is constantly discharging. The hospitality of our American neighbours is proverbial, and whenever it has been the good fortune of the Association to pass through their territory, it has been the recipient of kindnesses innumerable. Few who accompanied the party will forget their short sojourn in New York State a few years ago, the ovations at Syracuse and elsewhere, and the magnificent banquet at which the Canadians were entertained at Oswego by the corporation of that prosperous city."

Mr. John Cameron, like Mr. King, has vivid memories of the pleasantest kind when the Association, instead of as at present having a fixed meeting-place, was perambulatory in its habits. "There were," he says, "only five or six annual meetings held before I joined. I think my first meeting was at Brockville in 1865. M. Bowell, now Sir Mackenzie, was President that year. In 1867, when the annual meeting was at Goderich, I emerged from the obscurity of a full private as a member of the Executive Committee, and graduated through vice-presidencies to President in 1872 with the annual meeting at Bracebridge—a delightful trip, which really discovered the beauties of the Muskoka Lakes. I was also President in 1875, when we went to Philadelphia Exhibition, returning via New York. At New York we met Postmaster-General James, who was very kind. At Madison Square Gardens one evening the band played "God Save the Queen" in our honour. At the splendid New York post-office, the Postmaster-General made some of us speechify, the great dignitary adroitly assuring the massed staff that the principal officers of the Association were good Republicans, and ought to get a good reception—which we did get. In those years of the Association, the annual meetings were always held in midsummer, and were part of an annual excursion somewhere. The result was that the members acquired a great deal of valuable first-hand information respecting the geography and resources of the country. This information was disseminated. It was the custom to write extended letters to our own papers, giving full accounts of the trips with much interesting personal gossip and comment.

"One of the most delightful features of the meetings was the cultivation of the spirit of comradeship. In the earlier existence of the Association, political controversy was very strenuous, the lines were sharply drawn; there were few mugwumps: and there was in newspaper debate little beating about the bush. In Upper Canada there were two great personalities in public life—George Brown and John A. Macdonald. All good Reformers regarded 'John A.' as the incarnation of political evil; all good Conservatives paid analogous tribute to George Brown. Under these circumstances, it was what at first looked like a dubious experiment to form an Association comprising such antagonistic elements. But it worked out all right; delightful friendships were formed, and the foundation laid for those personal cordialities and intimacies among fellow-journalists which prevail in the Association to-day.

"The programmes of the annual meetings used to include an essay and a poem. Thus in 1867, at Goderich, John King (now K.C. of Toronto) was essayist, and David Wylie of the Brockville *Recorder* was poet; and a good, fervid Scotch-Canadian poet he was. I remember that at Cobourg in 1869 I was guilty of an essay, but I do not think it can be charged that I ever dropped into poetry. There were many delightful annual meetings and excursions, but I think that by common consent the most memorable and outstanding was that from Collingwood in 1868, to Fort William, via Georgian Bay, Lake Huron, and Lake Superior. William Buckingham, then of the Stratford *Beacon*, was President that year. The Executive took on board a hand-press and a quota of cases, sticks, and other printing necessities (type-setting at that period was all hand-setting); a small paper was published on board daily, very brightly edited by an editorial committee. In this little daily all sorts of pleasantries and ship gossip were set forth. The days were made enjoyable by stopping at various ports, while the nights were filled with music and recreations —a printed programme being furnished for each evening's performance. Steamships did not go so tiresomely fast in those days, and I think it took a glorious ten days or two weeks before we again touched Collingwood. The bright memories of that trip haunt us still."

IX.

A PRESIDENTIAL VERSE-MAKER.

But this anticipates a little the story of the Association subsequent to the Toronto meeting of 1863. it was decided to hold the next gathering at Belleville, and there the members assembled in November, 1864. This meeting is unique in that the President, Mr. David Wylie, delivered the annual address in verse. Familiar as the members probably were by this time with Mr. Wylie's facility in verse-making, one can picture their amazement when the jolly chairman unfolded his manuscript and delivered the following compound of humour and practical sense:

> Brethren of the Press, I greet you,
> Happy thus once more to meet you,
> To renew our kind fraternals,
> Free from all our young infernals!
> Whose capacious "copy" maw
> Never fills the "Devil's" jaw.
> Now, while off from impial bawlings,
> And all other sanctum callings—
> Let us con the year's proceedings,
> And the sum of our succeedings.
> Adding, too, our annual fruitings,
> By our pen and ink recruitings.

THE CANADIAN PRESS

Men of might, mission press-men,
Vigorous as college fresh-men;
Reading, aye, with pens and presses—
Despite frowns or vice-caresses,
Like old Britain's hardy seamen,
Guarding all that's dear to freemen;
Trouncing tyrants, lashing traitors,
And all ranks of England haters;
But to brother—those we love,
Gentle as the turtle dove.
Thus o'er heart-fonts scratched or battered,
Oil of love our band has scatter'd—
By the evil we help smother,
Ne'er retorting "you're another;"
But with —"Brother, oh, for shame,
Slur no brother's honest name."

Think you, craftsmen, in our banding,
We've not raised our social standing?
Curbed no devil in our steel-pin,
In our raids on brother Pressman,
When, with angry eyes a-glancing,
We have seen foe-sheets advancing;
Filled with ire, and hate, and passion,
A la mode Beelzebub-fashion.
Filled beside with lies and slander,
Say—has this not roused our dander?
And called up revengeful feeling,
Heart against all good thought steeling—
Till our Press Association,
Beamed out in its sublimation,
And withheld the taunting sneerer,

Or the back-cut lash server;
Pointing to the good old story
That the greatest act of glory
Is not found in blood-bought battles,
Storing up of lands or chattels,
Ships or houses, power or pelf,
But man ruling well himself.
So the greatest in our ken,
He who ruleth well his pen.

Startled thus from anger conning,
Heart a softer feeling donning,
Down the fire-pen would be dashed,
From the mind the hard word flashed,
To the goal of good-will floated—
There the bitter word be bloated,
And the lesson taught that never
Should we spurn "good Lord deliver."
Ne'er forget the glorious sentence,
Thus placed at our altar's entrance.
Brethren, print it for a warning,
Wear it for our heart's adorning.
Thus when evil tempting hover,
And good sense would play the rover,
Bring the truant to the traces,
Bind him in these golden braces—
Brother unto brother do—
All that you'd wish done to you.

Craftsmen, here in metre-hummings,
I confess my great short-comings,
That when Simcoe's Lake you paddl'd

Down to where are deep-sea soundings,
Where old ocean has its boundings;
Where the fog and mist discloses
Sturdy Britons in Blue Noses,
Where Nova Scotia and New Brunswick,
Gaze out on the wide Atlantic;
Where Prince Edward and Newfoundland,
Look to this our river boundland—
Dreaming we could be a nation,
By a great confederation,
That, united, none could scare us,
Sneer at, curse at, nor yet dare us;
That if backed by British Lion
To molest us none would try-on.

Since then all has been commotion,
Back has rolled the tide from ocean;
Delegates from tidal flowings
With Confederation glowings,
Have made inroads on our border,
Not with shot or shell disorder,
But with calm and peaceful feelings,
Waiting Canada's revealings;
Urging that a five-fold mingle
Stouter far is than a single;
That one foot on the Pacific,
Should excite no thought terrific,
And the other on th' Atlantic,
Ought to drive no neighbor frantic,
But be rather the inception
Of a jubilee conception
Hovering o'er, in animation,

GEO. SHEPPARD
A Member of First Executive
Committee, 1858

HON. THOMAS WHITE, P.C.
President 1864

THOS. SELLAR
President 1866

WM. BUCKINGHAM
President 1868

Birth-day of a free-born nation.
Politicians, patriots, placemen,
And all the other "fat-take" racemen,
Though not free from rank pollution,
Mingle in the revolution—
Evil for a time may prop-up—
Good men yet will reach the top-up.

Then the masses will be happy,
O'er their tea, o'er their nappy;
Then will come an age of wonder,
Then will slave chains burst asunder;
Then each man may be a caliph,
Fearing neither beak nor bailiff.
Money plenty, land for asking,
All be masters—none be tasking,
None dishonest, no wine-bibbers,
Printers have paid-up subscribers,
Sun aye shining, no rain drizzle—
If all ends not in a fizzle.

Brethren, herein much I've blended,
Now my yearly task is ended,
Scanning over every letter,
Some may think they could do better,
But, I pray, use charity,
Gift the greatest of the three.

What happened at the close of this noteworthy performance we are not told, but it imparts to the Belleville meeting an atmosphere of hilarity well fitted to
maintain the joyous character of these renewals of

4

friendships. Mr. Thomas White of the Hamilton *Spectator* was chosen President for the next convention, and Brockville was fixed upon as the rallying point for 1865. It was also resolved to hold an excursion at the close of the meeting. This magic word now appears in the annals for the first time.

X.

ANNUAL MEETINGS IN THE SIXTIES.

In Victoria Hall, Brockville, on September 5th, 1865, the members assembled. The prospect of an excursion had stimulated the attendance, and on the register the following names appear:

Thomas White, Jr., Hamilton *Spectator;* J. A. Campbell, Whitby *Gazette;* M. Bowell, Belleville *Intelligencer;* W. Gillespy, Hamilton, ex-President; Alex. Graham, Peterborough *Examiner;* W. H. Lawson, Peterborough; George Verrall, Strathroy *Dispatch;* E. Jackson, Newmarket *Era;* John Siddons, London *Prototype;* J. H. Wood, Sarnia *British Canadian;* A. McLachlan, *Home Journal*, St. Thomas; Thos. Willis, Belleville *Independent;* D. McDougall, Berlin, ex-President; G. W. McMullen, Picton *North American;* J. H. Gibson, Brantford *Expositor;* C. H. Hull, Hamilton *Times;* John Cameron, London *Advertiser;* Mr. Tiner, Toronto; W. T. Cox, Huron *Signal;* W. M. Nicholson, Barrie *Examiner;* J. S. Gurnett, Ingersoll *Chronicle;* A. J. Belch, St. Mary's *Argus;* W. R. Climie and Rev. J. R. Climie, Bowmanville *Statesman;* J. B. Abbott, St. Mary's *Standard;* O. V. VanDusen, Owen Sound *Comet;* Thomas Evans, London *Free Press;* R. McWhinnie, Woodstock *Sentinel;* D. Wylie,

Brockville *Recorder;* J. Somerville, Dundas *True Banner;* Robert Romaine, Peterborough *Review;* C. B. Robinson, *Canadian Post*, Lindsay; W. P. Kelly, *British Canadian*, Simcoe; W. Buckingham, Stratford *Beacon;* R. Boyle, Picton *Times;* G. L. Walker, Perth *Courier;* M. MacNamara, Perth *Courier;* J. Parnell, Kingston *Churchman;* J. King, Berlin *Telegraph;* W. J. Floyd, Cobourg *Star;* C. J. Hynes, Prescott *Messenger;* H. C. Kennedy, Morrisburg *Courier;* T. Sellar, Montreal *Echo;* T. S. Henry, J. R. Mason, Belleville *Chronicle;* Joseph Laing, Kincardine *Commonwealth;* R. Mathewson, Milton; William Kennedy, Napanee *Standard;* George Tye, Brampton *Times;* P. Burns, Prescott *Telegraph;* David Mathewson, Quebec *Gazette;* J. Larke, Oshawa *Vindicator;* James Lindsay, St. Thomas *Home Journal;* J. Louden, Berlin *Telegraph.*

President White's address was what might be expected from one of his force of character and sobriety of judgment. He referred to the closing of the Civil War in the United States as calling for renewed vigilance on the part of the newspaper men in the attitude they took on public questions. There was a danger of underestimating their power in influencing public opinion. He noted the improvement in the newspapers, not only for enterprise but for their gentlemanly forbearance.

"But a few years ago," he said, "topics of discussion between newspapers almost invariably before the third article degenerated into a mere personal quarrel between the editors, who were dragged by name into the arena, to the intense amusement of the worst class of the community and to the fostering of a wretched and unhealthy tone of public sentiment. To-day, let us be thankful for it, such discussions, like angel visits, are few and far between. And I think it is not too much to arrogate to the Press Association a large share of the merit of this improved tone. He who forgets what is due to the respectability of his profession and to the gentlemen who are engaged in it should be treated as an outlaw with whom no communion of any kind should be held."

Dealing with public men, he said that irrespective of politics altogether the press, if it would consult the public interests, should fairly and honorably recognize the claims which the public men of the country have upon its considerate and fair treatment. The press should cultivate a spirit of personal confidence between the people and the leaders of the people of whatever party. The Association, he continued, had done much good. It had made it a discreditable act for any newspaper writer to drag from behind the incognito of the press a brother journalist for the mere sake of gratifying prurient taste for mere personal vituperation.

On the day following the meeting, the Association left on a trip to Ottawa, going to Arnprior by the Brockville and Ottawa Railway and from there across Chats Lake by steamer. Then a delightful ride over the "horse" railway brought the company to Ottawa River, and after another boat trip, the pressmen were landed at Aylmer. At the latter place, the excursionists were met by Aldermen Cunningham, Mosgrove, and other gentlemen from Ottawa, with a goodly array of carriages to carry them over an excellent macadamized road of nine miles in length to Ottawa City. A stay of one day was made at the new capital, when the party left by train for Prescott, and from there made the trip by steamer through the rapids to Montreal. This was the first of a long series of delightful trips to various points of interest in Canada and the United States.

The assembling point in 1866 was Montreal. This was the first of three meetings held there. Mr. Bowell of the Belleville *Intelligencer* was President, and the attendance was the largest on record. The Western members went to Kingston by rail and then divided into two parties, one continuing by train to Montreal, the other descending the St. Lawrence rapids by the steamer "Grecian." In those days nearly all the islands in the river were finely wooded and the sportsman found the St. Lawrence both for fishing and duck shooting a veritable paradise, so that the modern traveller by the same route can scarcely realize the varied beauty of the scene forty years ago. The visitors nearly all stayed at the St. Lawrence Hall, which was then the chief hotel of Montreal, and although summer travel was at its height—for it was the month of August—the famous Mr. Hogan made his guests comfortable. Three Montreal journalists were elected members—Messrs. John Dougall, Chas. Heavysege, C. H. Kirby. On motion it was decided to drop the word "Upper," which had occasionally been used in the title of the Association.* The meeting lasted two hours, the members leaving for Quebec and vicinity, a picnic being given at Montmorency Falls.

* The society, as far as the writer can discover, was always styled by the name it now bears. It is so designated in the original cash book or ledger dated 1860. This motion adopted at Montreal is the only reference found to another title having been used.

XI.

THE EXCURSION TO THE NORTHERN LAKES.

THE Confederation year found the Association at Goderich, and to that distant point over fifty members travelled. President Sellar of Montreal was in the chair. The time was the month of August. The very date was a bold defiance of the party politicians, because the elections (it was before the day of simultaneous voting) for the first Parliament of Canada were still in progress. Mr. Sellar spoke patriotically of the birth of the new Dominion, an event which a few weeks before had been marked by the booming of cannon from the Gulf of St. Lawrence to Lake Superior. A new era, he pointed out, should dawn with the new nation, when broader sympathies and views would prevail, and men would call themselves Canadians rather than Nova Scotians and Ontarians. "I hope," he said, "to see in another year representatives from all parts of the Dominion present at our annual meeting." This was not the first expression of the wish. There are resolutions of years previous to 1867 urging members of the press in Quebec and the Maritime Provinces to join. Mr. Gillespy and others had often spoken of the desirability of having one Association for British North America. Doubtless actual steps had been taken although there is no accessible record of them. At this meeting Mr. Wylie moved to change the name to the British North America Press Association, but, we are told, after a discussion this was withdrawn and Mr. Gillespy's resolution to invite the editors of the Lower Provinces to join was carried. The press party were hospitably entertained by the municipal authorities of Goderich and an enjoyable excursion to East Saginaw, Saginaw City, and Bay City took place.

Having fixed upon a trip to Fort William, at the head of Lake Superior, as the great event of 1868, the town of Collingwood was chosen as the meeting place. There was a large attendance. In the list of those present are found the names of J. A. Campbell, Whitby *Gazette*, who was President for the year; W. Buckingham, James Young, M.P., David Wylie, Wm. Gillespy, W. R. Climie, E. Jackson, John Cameron, R. Boyle, James Somerville, P. E. W. Moyer, H. Hough, C. Blackett Robinson, John King, J. S. Larke, W. F. Luxton (then editor of the Strathroy *Age*), A. H. St. Germain, Alex. McLean, W. Bristow (of Montreal), J. W. Conger, W. McIntosh, D. McDougall, R. Romaine, M. Provencher (of *La Minerve*), W. J. Higgins, E. R. Dewhurst, Geo. Tye, R. Matheson, Thomas Messenger. Mr. Campbell's address was full of patriotism and his references to the new Canada and its great opportunities were enthusiastically applauded. The members adopted this resolution:

"This Association begs to express its deep sorrow at the untimely death of the late Thomas D'Arcy McGee, a talented member of our fraternity."

E. JACKSON
President 1870

R. MATHISON
Sec'y-Treas. 1871

REV. W. F. CLARKE
President 1873

H. HOUGH
President 1874

Not long before, as we have seen, Mr. McGee had referred in appreciative terms to the Association and its power to expound and dignify the mission of the press. He had attended the London meeting and was on friendly terms with many of the members. He fell, by the hand of an assassin, at Ottawa, April 6th, 1868.

Mr. Wylie was the poet at Collingwood, and made some happy hits as usual:

"God bless the new Dominion, pray we all;
God bless our people, be they great or small;
Bless her broad lakes, her forests and her fields,
Bless all the produce the Dominion yields.
Grant her long peace, and distant be the day
When swords are drawn and scabbards thrown away:
Live and let live, our motto, as we go,
Never intruding—never fearing foe.
And bless our rulers, for they want it much,
Especially the Irish, French, and Dutch;
For Britons in their lofty pride and ease
Think themselves bless'd—'Britannia rules the waves,'
Therefore no blessing want; but this is fudge,
For no men need it more—if I'm to judge."

Business having been disposed of, and it was not burdensome, preparations were made for the voyage up the lakes. The members had already travelled over the Northern Railway to Collingwood and had been overwhelmed with civilities and attentions by Hon. John Beverley Robinson, the President, and Colonel Cumberland, the Manager of the line. A special train was theirs and the directors' car contained several distinguished guests, including Hon. John Sandfield Macdonald, Prime Minister of Ontario. There was a reception at Barrie, when addresses were delivered by Judge Gowan (now Sir James Gowan) and Wm. Lount, M.P.P. (in later times M.P. for Centre Toronto and a judge of the High Court). At Collingwood the Mayor and Corporation gave the Association a banquet. Next day, Saturday, July 11th, 1868, the party embarked on the "Algoma," and the memorable excursion began. A printing press and type were taken on board with the intention of printing a daily newspaper during the voyage. A file of this great organ of steamboat opinion has been preserved. The chief editor was W. M. Nicholson and the general manager W. R. Climie. The first issue of "The Canadian Press" gave the place of honour to the following stanzas:

Go forth precursor of a better time,
   Go like the dove from Noah's Ark of old;   .
Stay not, rest not, till o'er this rugged clime
   Thou leav'st a power more precious far than gold.

Tell of this land of rocky isles and plains—
   Keen messengers are now upon its track,
Lo! scan its mines, its varied fruits and grains,
   And take the winnow'd jewels with them back.

The paper promptly claimed to have "the largest circulation of any journal published on a steamboat in America," and advertisers were requested to note the fact. In consequence there was a rush of advertising. Telegrams for publication were received by

"Lake Superior Submarine Line" and included such interesting news as the following:—

TORONTO, *July* 15, 1868.

The *Globe's* correspondent makes the startling announcement that he saw a man who heard another man say there was great indignation at Ottawa because three Ministers had gone outside the city limits for a drive. Great sensation in Toronto.

A painful tragedy of a Toronto citizen (moving in the highest circles) who cut his throat with a bar of soap turned out to be grossly exaggerated, as later accounts showed that he had purchased the soap for domestic purposes.

Cable news of vast import was published. The Paris correspondent said:—

The Emperor Napoleon has decided to invite the Canadian Press Association to Paris. They will be entertained at dinner at St. Cloud, if they do not arrive on Wednesday, which is washing day.

The chronicles of each day's proceedings reflect much jollity and enjoyment, until, a week later, the "Algoma" steamed into Collingwood again and the party separated. The *Canadian Press*, which thus "suspended publication" after six issues, declared the trip to be the most pleasurable ever undertaken by the members. It might be remarked, as one explanation of this, that the lakes were smooth and the weather warm.

XII.

BLANDISHMENTS FROM OVER THE BORDER.

THE era of summer excursions was now at its height; the idea of a business convention for discussions of a trade and a professional character being relegated to a secondary and minor place in the annual programme. The President's address, the annual essay, and the annual poem provided the literary part of each entertainment. The quality of these contributions was of a high order. In years to come the Association was to lay less stress upon the purely literary side of the press as an avocation, until in 1907, Mr. Preston, M.P.P., temperately and sagaciously reminded the members that there is a moral as well as a commercial basis to the profession. During the period under review no such warning was needed. The presidential addresses were admirable. Neither given over to platitude and rhapsody, nor full of the vivacious maxims of the counting room, they proclaimed the high principles which should govern a healthy and influential journalism. In 1869 the Association met at Cobourg, and President Buckingham's address once more struck the key-note of the Association's purpose. He pointed out that the day was past when men bred to the other professions could hold journalism in light esteem. In such men as Joseph Howe and Thomas D'Arcy McGee great natural gifts and high literary culture were displayed. There was at home and abroad a conviction of the potency of the press as a moral agent and popular educator. "It is," he continued, "fitting that in no spirit of vainglorious boasting, but with earnestness of mind, as men feeling the weight of the responsibility cast upon them, we should at times recall considerations such as these with the endeavour to make ourselves worthy of our vocation. Journalistic effort has already attained a high degree of excellence in Canada, but the readiness of the people to acknowledge and encourage the enterprise of newspaper conductors should stimulate us to fresh exertions."

The proceedings of 1869 partook of an international character. After meeting on July 20th, selecting Mr. Wylie as President for the coming year, and being hospitably entertained by the town council, the party were taken to Rice Lake, and in the evening gave a conversazione at Cobourg. Next day the steamer "Norseman" carried the members across Lake Ontario to Rochester. This was a time when the good feeling between Canada and the United States was disturbed. The termination of the Reciprocity Treaty by Congress, the threatened recurrence of the Fenian Raids, the bad relations between Great Britain and the Republic over the Alabama depredations, combined to create high tension. No trace of this was observable in the splendid reception given the Canadians at Rochester. An entertaining narrative of the trip has survived. When the visitors reached the Central depot, the Zouaves' band struck up "God Save the Queen," and "Yankee Doodle" followed in due course. Carriages took the party to see all the principal sights during the afternoon and evening. They were everywhere greeted with cordiality and their pathway bestrewn with flowers. Speeches of welcome and fraternal greetings were made by Mayor Smith for the corporation and citizens of Rochester; by Mr. James of the *Democrat*, for the Rochester press; and by Mr. Buckingham and Mr. Wylie for the Canadians. Complaint is made in the Canadian newspapers of that time that the late hours with His Worship of Rochester and his friends gave the visitors too little time for sleep, in view of the engagements made for them at Syracuse and Oswego. They managed, however, to reach the former city in time next day for a hospitable entertainment at the hands of their brethren of the Syracuse press, who had provided a luncheon graced by the Mayor and Mayoress and other prominent people. A special train from Oswego was too soon in waiting at Syracuse to take the Canadians to that city, in charge of a large deputation. In Oswego, carriages were ready to convey them to various places and to bring them back at five o'clock to the rink, where there was a big dinner, followed by a grand ball. The London *Advertiser* thus spoke of the event:

"A grand banquet was laid in the rink, which was decorated in magnificent style with evergreens and flowers, devices in gas jets, streamers, English and American flags, mottoes, etc. The spread was superb. Nothing that the tropics or temperate zones could produce to grace the tables seemed lacking. The speeches were eloquent and fraternal. The ball, to a late hour in the evening, was dazzlingly brilliant. About a thousand persons were present."

The Canadians left about midnight by steamer for Kingston, where an address was read by the Mayor, and suitably responded to. There was plenty to engage attention in the invitations of this place until the hour came for embarkation for Belleville by way of the Bay of Quinte. At Picton, it is said, the inhabitants turned out *en masse*. At 11 p.m., when they got to Belleville, the excursionists found that the local journalists had provided a fine repast at the Dafoe House. The chair was ably filled by Mr. Diamond, police magistrate, and the vice-chairs by Mr. Mason, of the *Chronicle*, and Mr. Shepherd, of the *Intelligencer*. Though the hour was late some excellent speeches were made. Mr. Shepherd said Mr. Mackenzie Bowell, who took a deep interest in the Association, wished him to state that imperative business had taken him to England, thus depriving him of the pleasure he had anticipated of entertaining his newspaper friends at his own residence.

The Stratford *Beacon* of July 20, 1869, draws a moral from the profuseness of the attentions bestowed upon the Canadians during their visit to the American cities. It says that when it was determined to include Rochester, Syracuse, and Oswego in the excursion programme for the year, it was not for a moment thought that such demonstrations would await them. They expected to be allowed to move quickly along, with the time allotted to their stay at their own disposal. But the contrary was the case. At the Convention in

Detroit on the Reciprocity Treaty a coercive policy was recommended to be tried against Canada with a view to bringing her into the Union. That had failed. And now a persuasive course was followed. The purpose was avowed at the Oswego dinner of making the Canadians willing "captives." Their right hand, the American speakers said in effect, was a maimed member, and Canada was the finger wanting to make it perfect. "It was hard for guests thus feted and flattered to resist such blandishments. But they had the courage to say 'No.' They told their American hosts that there could be a reciprocity of trade as well as of good feeling without a political union, that the Canadian love of British institutions was more than one of mere sentiment—and that if a free interchange of commodities could not be had except at the cost of annexation, Canada must content herself by living without it. They were reminded, too, that we had enjoyed a high degree of prosperity since the repeal of the treaty, and that Canada would never humble herself by going on her knees before the people at Washington to beg for its renewal. Whatever designs the Americans may have had upon us in the splendid reception accorded the representatives of our newspapers, we cannot but think that the meetings which have taken place will have a beneficial effect in more ways than one. And not the least of the many advantages resulting from our free intercourse with our neighbors will be the removal of many misconceptions which had hitherto obscured their minds and the imparting to them of a right understanding of the true feelings of Canadians in regard to the kind of intercourse which they believed ought to exist between the two countries." Reverting again to the subject, Miss Maple Leaf is made to say to Brother Jonathan:

> You need not come wooing to me,
> For my heart, *my heart, is over the sea.*

5

XIII.

AN ADDRESS FROM THE HON. GEORGE BROWN.

FLUSHED with triumph, and resolving to keep up the pace or perish in the attempt, each succeeding Executive vied with its predecessor in providing an excursion programme that would attract a large attendance. There was a certain amount of peril in this policy, as we shall presently see, but for the moment all went well. Brantford was the rendezvous for 1870, and the date selected, July 19th. There was an address from the Mayor and Corporation and a drive about the city and out to Bow Park Farm, the estate of Hon. George Brown. The poetical President, Mr. Wylie, recited some verses in lieu of the annual message from the chair, and Mr. John Maclean, of the *People's Journal,* Hamilton, read an essay which exhibited a clear comprehension of the newspaper situation in Canada. Mr. Maclean was emphatic in proclaiming the responsibilities of the press in Canada in keeping the peace, —a warning rendered the more piquant by the strong indignation then felt at the second invasion of Canada by the Fenian raiders.

At the banquet in the evening, Hon. George Brown delivered a distinctly political address. But there is no evidence that the Conservative editors present either fainted in their chairs or foamed at the mouth. But the speech is undoubtedly more partizan than a public man would deliver now before the Association. But Mr. Brown was a Reformer or nothing. If he had had to re-cast the Westminster Confession, he would have added a clause endorsing the Reform party. Coming from so eminent a man, however, the speech is noteworthy, and this is the *Expositor's* summary of it:—

"The Hon. George Brown, replying to the toast to the Dominion of Canada, said: There was no toast to which he would so gladly reply as that of the Dominion of Canada. As he had not appeared on any public occasion for three years, he thought it was so much the more necessary that his words should be few and well chosen. After twenty years' struggling for the interests of the people of Western Canada—after battling for so long that justice might be done for us—that we might have the constitutional right of self-government —he claimed that he had a perfectly legitimate right to reply on this occasion. What was the reason that our Customs duties were now 25 per cent. less than before Confederation? That we have now $3,000,000 of surplus in our treasury? John Sandfield Macdonald takes credit to himself for his great surplus, but it was the measure of Confederation that accomplished it, a measure which John Sandfield opposed with all his might, both tooth and nail. We have a Government of Ontario to thank for collecting and taking care of this money, but not for the surplus itself.

"This scheme has obtained all that could be desired for the people—it is not responsible for the legislation in the North-West or for the winding route of the Intercolonial; but the Cabinet of the Dominion are accountable to the people for this. The framers of the Act of Confederation have obtained for the people of Canada the full power of governing themselves, if they like to exercise it; if the people want bad government they can have it; if they want good government, it lies with them, and them alone, to procure it. The resources and wealth of the Province have materially increased since the union of the Provinces; there are now millions of money in the country seeking investment. The honorable gentleman deprecated strongly this discussion of the question of the independence of the Dominion, which was beginning to rise. It is perfect nonsense for any man of sense to talk about the benefits which would accrue by separation from the Mother Country. Have we not now a perfect right of self-government, while England carries out our diplomatic relations for us, and is ready at any moment to defend us by the whole power of the army and navy? —thus relieving us of the necessity of keeping up a standing army. Britain has spent a large amount of money upon us, then let us not take umbrage at a few cross words from Downing Street; whatever may be the opinions of Granville or Gladstone, there is no doubt that the great broad mind of the people of England is in favour of keeping up colonial connection. We have got a better system of government than can be found on the face of the earth; better than England, for kings and queens must die, and others may rise in their stead who may endeavor to overturn the liberties of the people; better than the republic; for although a President only holds office for four years he appoints his own Cabinet and rules with the power of the dictator. In our present circumstances we want more than an economic administration; we want statesmanship and a commercial policy to develop the mighty resources of this great Dominion. It is our pride that we have no noble class who live on and above the people. From Gaspé to Sandwich every man is expected to earn his bread and his reputation by the labour of his hands, and the abilities which God has given him. Mr. Brown closed a very able speech by referring to the proposed union of British Columbia with the Dominion, and hoped that it would not be completed with too much haste or we would likely have a repetition of the troubles in Nova Scotia and the North-West."

Mr. Erastus Jackson was elected President at Brantford, and it is interesting to note the names which now begin to figure at the meetings. Old stagers like Mr. Gillespy and Mr. McDougall still continue to put in an appearance and one finds among the new men: N. King, Barrie; E. J. B. Pense, Kingston; Alex. McLean, Cornwall; James Shannon, Kingston; G. R. Pattullo, Woodstock; J. G. Buchanan, Hamilton; David Creighton, Owen Sound; J. McMullen, Brockville; W. R. Climie, Bowmanville; J. H. Hacking, Listowel; E. C. Campbell, Cayuga; A. H. Dymond, Toronto; C. J. Beeman, Newburg. From Brantford, the members went to Buffalo, where the editorial fraternity of the city, headed by Messrs. Chester, *Courier*, Warren, *Commercial*, Larned & Ferris, *Express*, and Bryan, *Post*, were cordial and attentive. The party went by boat to Cleveland, where they were given a dinner, and then to Windsor, taking the Great Western to London. At London a local committee gave the visitors an enjoyable time.

Assembling in Toronto July 18th, 1871, the Association heard Mr. Jackson's practical address, which contained a suggestion that has since been so potent a factor in determining the programmes of the annual meetings. He said:

"It is thought by many members of our Association that more time should be allowed for our annual meetings—thus affording opportunity for full and free discussion of such subjects of a practical character as may have a direct bearing upon the profession. With this view I very largely concur, and confidently express the hope that in making arrangements for future gatherings this object will be kept in view."

Whether or not the pale spectre of brisk discussions upon machine composition, foreign advertising rates, and country correspondents flitted before the eyes of the members it is impossible to say. All we know from the record is that excursion plans for the following year were at once taken up and the party embarked on the "Banshee," that ancient steamer familiar to St. Lawrence River travellers, and began the journey to Montreal. From Montreal the route was by Ottawa River to the Capital, where the various points of interest were inspected.

The serene indifference of the Association for such trifles as general elections has already been noted. This was well exemplified in 1872. Parliament was dissolved on July 8th of that year, and on the 10th, the members were at Bracebridge for their annual convention. While Sir John Macdonald waged a desperate fight vainly trying to prevent the Province of Ontario from slipping away from him ("Had I not taken regularly to the stump," he wrote to a friend, "we should have been completely routed") the members of the Association were sailing through the Muskoka Lakes enjoying the ideal scenery of that region. The address of President Somerville was a model of practical sense. An extract will illustrate the sturdy independence of tone that characterized his utterances.

"During the past few years a very marked improvement has been observed in the advertising columns of our local newspapers—many having altogether shut out the quack ads. which were inserted at half price, and were at the same time a disgrace and pestilence to the community in which they were circulated. Publishers should have but one rule in dealing with advertisers. All should be treated alike, whether local or foreign. One price alone should be charged—as it is decidedly unfair to give an outsider advertising, an advantage over the one who is a steady customer and resides in the locality where the paper is published. And further, the system of indiscriminate 'puffing' which some journalists indulge in is a disgrace to the profession. Advertisers should be allowed to do their own 'puffing' and be made to pay for it if they must have it. The local columns of a newspaper should not be prostituted for the purpose of declaring week in and week out that this or that man sells very fine Young Hyson, very rich old cheese, or very rare old rum. Some newspaper men appear to live with the sole idea in view that they must never cease puffing those who advertise in their columns, and in time their puffs become nauseous in the extreme to their readers—who very justly refuse to be influenced thereby, and finally lose all respect for the editor and his newspaper. This evil exists to a very great extent also with regard to notices of public entertainments, and other passing events. Editors should be honest in their criticisms. They should be candid and truthful in all things. And no one who appears in public should receive favourable mention unless he or she is justly entitled to it. A newspaper conducted on these principles cannot fail to be appreciated and respected by a discerning public, and will secure an influence thereby which could be attained in no other way."

Judging by the descriptive letters sent by the editors to their papers, the Muskoka excursion was a great success. It "discovered" to many Canadians the beautiful scenery and health-giving breezes of that famous region. Mr. John Cameron was elected President, and among the new members "sworn in" were: W. M. Hale, Orillia; F. Britton, Gananoque; R. Herring, Petrolea; H. Watt, Meaford; C. D. Barr, Toronto; N. Burns, Georgetown; F. J. Gissing, Woodstock.

JOHN CAMERON
President 1872 and 1875

C. D. BARR
President 1876

W. R. CLIMIE
Sec.-Treas., 1876-1889

JAMES INNES
President 1877

XIV.

AN INTERREGNUM OF DEPRESSION.

THERE was no excursion in 1873. It is not easy to discover the cause, except that the railways were not as ready as usual to make suitable rates, and there are signs that the companies were disposed to raise the question of the newspaper status of those who took part in the excursions. The Executive decided to assemble in London on September 24th during the meeting of the Association's old friend the Provincial Exhibition. President Cameron's address contained a pointed allusion to the employment of personalities by newspapers, showing that the press was being dragged into the virulent party discussions which raged throughout Canada during this year and the next, over the Pacific Scandal. Politics were once more very bitter. The great Conservative party were out of office. During two decades they had only held power for 18 years and naturally felt exclusion to be unjust and tyrannical. Mr. Bengough drew an unfeeling cartoon in *Grip* depicting these persecuted men with mourning bands and long streamers to their hats. Altogether it was a melancholy time. Probably there were other influences at work to sap the vitality of the Association. For several years the members had carried out a series of excursions that must have imposed a heavy burden of work upon the committee in charge. The places of interest most easily available had all been visited and to discover others was a difficult task. The country was entering upon the severe commercial depression which held the chief countries of the world in thrall for some time. A slight, but undeniable reaction had set in, affecting both the work and the membership of the Association. So much so that when Rev. W. F. Clarke, the President for 1874, called the members together in the York County Council Chambers, Toronto, in July, there were just twenty-five persons in attendance. The chairman's theme was "the present state of our organization." It brings to mind Pitt moving the British House of Commons into committee to consider the state of the nation. Mr. Clarke probed the wound with merciless severity in order to vitalize and nourish the Association for the future. He recommended that the address be considered a confidential statement to the members for the purpose of prescribing a remedy, and not to proclaim to a sneering world the ills that afflicted the society. The address was referred to a committee consisting of Messrs. Somerville, Innes, Climie, Hough, and King, and it is to their lasting renown that the Association took a new lease of life and has never since suffered from even temporary paralysis. After the meeting was over, a small party left for Collingwood and took a trip to Duluth and back by the steamer "Cumberland."

To Hamilton, rich with memories of Gillespy and the hearty hospitalities of the early days, the Association hied in 1875. There, in the City Council Chamber, President Hough delivered the opening address. It was optimistic in tone. "While many other branches of industry are suffering from the present financial depression," he said, "I believe the members of the fourth estate experience little or no perplexity in their business concerns." The importance of the Association to the press fraternity generally was dwelt upon. Party politics flourished in the Dominion even more keenly than in the United States, and this had led to much rancorous discussion. This was to be deprecated, and the Association existed to bring about an improved state of feeling. The President's sensible and kindly address was duly appreciated. So, too, were the excellent arrangements of the local committee for the enjoyment and comfort of the visitors. The party were entertained at the residence of Mr. John Eastwood, of the *Times*. They also went to the home of Mr. George Tuckett, where Mr. Somerville made a happy speech. They visited Hon. Isaac Buchanan at "Auchmar," and Mr. James Turner at "Highfield," and after making some other calls, left by steamer for the Niagara River and spent the night at the Queen's Royal, as the guests of Mr. Winnett. The Falls, Buffalo, Navy Island, Chippewa, and the various places in that historic region were all visited. Hon. Edward Goff Penny, of the Montreal *Herald*, having joined the party for an hour or two, was appropriately made an honorary member. Among the new members at this meeting in 1875 was Mr. Goldwin Smith, who subsequently became a vice-president of the Association and who lent the powerful aid of his literary fame and sociable qualities to the organization for many a year.

XV.

THE ASSOCIATION AND MR. GOLDWIN SMITH.

IN its treatment of Mr. Goldwin Smith, the Association proved staunch to the principle laid down from the first: that political controversy was never to interfere with personal friendship or the respect due from one member to another. The presence of this distinguished man of letters in Canada was a fortunate circumstance. How he came to fix his residence here has been thus explained by himself:

"I held the Professorship of Modern History at Oxford—the chair held before by Arnold, and since by Freeman and Stubbs—which was the summit of my limited ambition. I resigned it because family reasons obliged me to leave Oxford, requiring my presence at home. On my father's death, having independent means and no profession, I was rather at a loss for an object in life. I was offered a nomination to Parliament, and for a sure seat; but I knew I had neither strength for the work nor any gifts that way. I had visited America and had formed an interest in American history and politics which has since led to my writing a little history of the United States. My thoughts were turned that way when I fell in with Andrew D. White, then President of the Cornell University, which was being founded under his own and other very noble auspices for the special benefit of poor students. White invited me to take part as a historical lecturer in the enterprise. Two very happy, and I hope not unfruitful, years I spent at Cornell, with which I maintain a more than friendly connection. Then I took up my abode with members of my family who had settled before me here, and presently I married and became permanently resident in Canada."*

There was nothing of condescension or patronage in his manner of connecting himself with the Association. For more than thirty years, either as active or honorary member, Mr. Goldwin Smith has identified himself with every effort made by the organization to promote the higher interests of the press. He has spoken many a word of wise counsel at the annual meetings. Never obtrusive, but always fearless in impressing upon journalists their responsibilities and obligations, his has been a good influence. It is unnecessary to recall his participation in such literary or journalistic work as brought him into close contact with the Canadian press. In the *Canadian Monthly* and the *Week*, in the publication of *The Bystander*, and latterly in the *Weekly Sun*, Mr. Goldwin Smith has contributed much to the formation of public opinion. Having set and kept a high standard, his example has naturally been a powerful factor—how powerful we are too near his time to determine. But his attainments and rank in the literary world justify the pride of the Canadian Press Association in claiming him as a conspicuous illustration of the triumph of its aim

* Toronto Mail and Empire, Feb. 2, 1899.

and purpose. He joined in 1875, and attended the Hamilton meeting in that year. His health was proposed and his speech in reply—so the faithful minute book records—was "in his happiest vein." He consented to read an essay at the convention of 1876. This duty he duly performed. In the course of this remarkable essay he expressed the following opinion:

"One other point must be mentioned, as it has special reference to the Association at the kind bidding of which this paper has been written. It would be a great thing if by such Associations as this, or in any other way, we could give to journalism the character and tone of a regular profession. It would be a great thing for journalists themselves. For the public, because professional opinion is always a strong support of individual probity, and has saved many a lawyer from tripping, when left to his own moral strength he would have fallen. For the journalists themselves, because membership of a body which affords such guarantees could not fail to be, like membership of other honorable professions, an additional title to social respect. The legal, medical, and military professions are thoroughly organized; they can make their rules, enforce them against offenders, and in the last resort purge their order of anyone who has flagrantly disgraced it. In the case of journalism it would be very difficult to bring into existence an organization of this kind, especially while we are divided by party, which would too surely prevent the journalists of one party from concurring in the repression of outrage committed against a journalist of the other party. Still, meetings like the present may produce something of a professional feeling;

enough to make journalists conscious of the fact that
they have a corporate interest in the position, rights,
and privileges of their order; enough to make them,
when these rights and privileges are violated, lay party
feeling in some measure aside and sympathize with the
aggrieved, not with the aggressor; enough, if not to
put down tyrannical ruffianism, at least to subject it
to some measure of control."

It was natural that Mr. Goldwin Smith should be
embroiled, at one period or another, with the party
politicians. He was independent of both sides and he
sought no favours. At different times, therefore, he
was attacked by Reformers and by Conservatives. In
1881, the Association decided to offer him, on the eve
of a visit to England, the compliment of a public banquet. This was, if for no other reason, an appropriate
recognition of his friendship for the Association. He
had, during the previous year, given the press the
splendid example of journalistic vigour and literary
excellence embodied in *The Bystander*. He had been
an officer of the Association and was on terms of kindly
intimacy with its members. The proposal was cor-
dially received on all sides. The dinner was given
at the Queen's Hotel, Toronto, on June 3rd, 1881,
and Mr. J. B. Trayes, of Port Hope, the President for
the year, occupied the chair. Some of the leading newspaper writers and literary men of Toronto joined with
the members of the Association in arranging the affair,
which was most successful. Mr. Goldwin Smith's
reply* to the toast to his health was, like his essay in
1876, a brilliant disquisition upon the functions,

* Published in full in the Canadian Monthly for July, 1881.

status, and duties of the press. He began with a reference to the society which entertained him on that occasion:

"The Press Association, which does me the honour to entertain me to-night, is a non-political organization. Around this table are gentlemen of all opinions, with some of whom I have the honour to disagree on almost all important subjects. Here is the Tory lion lying down—I was going to say with the Grit lamb— with the Grit tiger (laughter)—while the lamb of independent journalism (cheers and laughter) remains unhurt between them. Gentlemen, I hope this evening's meeting is something much better than a tribute to any particular individual. I hope it is a manifestation of the fraternity of the press. I hope its meaning is that amidst all our political differences, and all the conflicts into which daily, weekly and monthly we are hurried, we are still members of a brotherhood, we are still an honourable and powerful profession, which has its own rules, its own courtesies, privileges, and duties —a profession which will uphold and protect its members in the fair and conscientious exercise of their calling, which will honour those who bring it credit, and withhold honour from those who bring it discredit." (Cheers.)

This address was crowded with apt and telling allusions to the various phases of newspaper life. It exhibited a perfect comprehension of the difficulties of a journalist's lot, and the practical conditions under which he does his work. Referring to the difference between journalism and literature as an art, Mr. Goldwin Smith delivered this interesting opinion upon the product of a newspaper writer, as compared with the more pretentious achievement of an author of books:

"There are people who say that to be a journalist and to be nothing are things not incompatible. I have candid friends who say, 'Why do you go into journalism? You ought to write a book; the only way to make yourself immortal and to become a benefactor to society is to write a book.' Well, considering the ponderous contents of our bookstores, and the voluminous catalogues which bookworms, such as I am, receive, perhaps the title of a benefactor of society might be claimed, in a modest way, by the man who does not write a book. I suppose it may be true that, as a student, I did set out in life to write a book, I suppose that was my manifest destiny, but, like other manifest destinies, it was not fulfilled. I was taken away from my college early in life, became mixed up with public men, and was at length drawn into the press. So I became a journalist, and a journalist I have remained; though I came to Canada not with the slightest intention of going on the press, least of all on the political press, which for some time, in fact, I steadfastly eschewed. I thought only of making a home for myself among my relatives; but I was drawn in by the current of national life which began to flow after Confederation in the intellectual as well as in the political sphere. I did not complain of my lot. It is perfectly true that the works of a journalist are ephemeral; they go into the nether world of old files and are forgotten. But does not the same fate befall a good many books? Look at the back shelves of any great library. What

6

a necropolis of the immortals is there. There, amidst inviolate dust and cobwebs which are never disturbed, sleep great masters of the civil law who were once as gods for their wisdom. There sleep the authors of many a system of philosophy which now has no disciples. There sleep the authors of many a system of science which has been superseded a hundred times by the advance of modern thought. The fact is, that to be immortal you must not only have an undying genius, but an undying subject. Shakespeare, Homer, Cervantes, had undecaying subjects, but some doubt whether even they are now what they were to their contemporaries. We all wish to survive our ashes in a certain sense, but not to one in millions is it given to be really immortalized by literature."

In the history of the Association there is no better evidence of the sincerity and vitality of its earliest professions than its attitude toward this great English man of letters who had, to use his own expression, "brought to Canadian journalism the fruits of a life spent, to a great extent, in political and historical study and among statesmen."

CHAPTER XVI.

TRIP TO THE MARITIME PROVINCES.

WHEN the time came for the 1876 meeting the prosperity of the Association once more stood out in bold relief. It had weathered the storm, and was about to open a fresh period of activity and success. When President Cameron opened the annual meeting at noon on June 30th, 1876, in the York County Council Chambers, Toronto, he gazed upon a numerous and influential company. Among the old members were Wm. Gillespy, Goldwin Smith, Erastus Jackson, A. Matheson, John Maclean, W. Watt, Jr., H. Hough, James Shannon, W. R. Climie, C. D. Barr, C. Blackett Robinson, James Somerville, John King, J. G. Buchanan, J. W. Walker, and a host of others. The new members ballotted in included: J. B. Trayes, Port Hope; Wm. Houston, Toronto; W. Weld, London; J. W. Bengough, Toronto; L. K. Cameron, London; A. J. Matheson, Perth; George Eyvell, Toronto; W. T. Sawle, Caledonia; S. P. Panton, Milton, and others equally well known. Mr. Cameron took for his subject "The Liberty of the Press; its Uses and Abuses," and analyzed with skill the functions of the newspapers; their political leadership, their position as purveyors of information, their power to educate, the responsibility conferred by impersonal journalism. He contended stoutly for liberty, and argued that the evils of "occasional licence" were more than counterbalanced by the benefits of untrammeled debate. The address was refreshingly fearless. Its sentiments are as apposite to conditions to-day as to those of thirty years ago. Mr. Goldwin Smith followed with an essay in his own brilliant style. A quotation from this paper has already been given. It may suffice to remark here that none of Mr. Goldwin Smith's numerous allusions to the journalistic calling equals in skilful analysis the essay of 1876. The Association transacted one or two satisfactory items of business before leaving for Philadelphia to visit the Centennial Exposition. Arrangements were made to receive into full membership the Dominion Editors and Reporters' Association, a body which had evinced a wish to join the parent organization. A letter was read from Hon. Alexander Mackenzie, Prime Minister of Canada, inviting the members to take their next excursion over the Intercolonial Railway. The "Southern Belle" conveyed the party to Niagara and they went to Philadelphia by the Lehigh Valley Railroad. Of the enjoyments of this trip, which included a visit to New York, Mr. Cameron has briefly spoken. While in Philadelphia, staying at the Merchant's Hotel, the members gave much attention to the interests of the Association. Like the spouse of John Gilpin, though on pleasure bent, they had a frugal mind. A new system of electing members was drafted to meet the requirements of the railways, which desired to confer privileges only upon active members of the press. The plan adopted is that substantially

in force to-day. The annual fee was made payable
in advance; each new name proposed was to be nom-
inated and vouched for by two members. Only those
engaged as editors, publishers, or printers were eligible
for membership.

The people of the Maritime Provinces have long
been famous for the sterling quality of their hospitality
and friendship. When the Canadian Press Association accepted Premier Mackenzie's invitation to visit
that portion of the Dominion by travelling over the
Intercolonial the members must have had some idea
of the kindness with which they would be received.
But realization surpassed expectation. Mr. C. D.
Barr, of the Lindsay *Post*, was President, and the place
at which the members assembled for the 1877 meeting
was Montreal. There on August 1st the annual
address was delivered. Mr. Barr developed the idea
that had at previous meetings found favor with many
members—the utilization of the Association for purposes of business as well as pleasure. He reminded
the gathering that this view had been held by the founders of the Society, and that much benefit could be de-
rived by a business convention to discuss sound methods in publishing. So highly did his listeners approve
of the President's suggestions, which were not of a
theoretical kind, but abounded in carefully thought
out details, that on the way down to the Atlantic shores
brisk discussions were carried on. Although no record
of the debates is available, it does not appear that the
conferences differed greatly from those which are now-
adays taken down by expert stenography and embalmed
in the annual report. A number of resolutions endors-

ing Mr. Barr's views were adopted. One or two features of the meeting may be noted. The new constitution was adopted. Mr. Wylie, of Brockville, having retired from active journalism, was transferred to the honorary list.

The excursionists went first to Prince Edward Island, where a delegation of the local press acted as hosts. They next moved on to Nova Scotia. The President recalls an interesting detail of the trip. "Mr. C. J. Brydges," he says, "was manager of the Intercolonial Railway at the time, and was courteous and painstaking in all arrangements for the success of the excursion and the comfort of the party. Are not all the doings and sayings, the speeches and hospitalities duly recorded in the chronicles—daily or weekly—reposing in bound volumes in each newspaper printing office awaiting the eager eye and willing hand of the modern historiographer of the Press Association? Our reception was most hospitable. About a hundred miles or so from Halifax, as our train was speeding to the eastern capital, we were met by a bright and engaging young man who was then city editor of the Halifax *Chronicle*. He came on to give us a true Nova Scotian welcome and to see that everything was just right. He became immediately popular with the men as well as with the ladies—he was clever enough to be just as nice to the old ladies as to the young ones. He was particularly eloquent about the attractions of Halifax, the beauties of the "North-West Arm"—that lovely bay that is one of the chief attractions of the Nova Scotian capital, and, if my memory does not play me false at this long distance of time, I think he had some

views as to the superiority of Halifax over St. John as
an ocean port, but I am not sure about this. This
attractive young man, not many years afterwards,
became Premier of Nova Scotia, and then Finance
Minister of Canada. This is mentioned for the encouragement of other bright young reporters who may
go out to welcome the Press Association excursionists
in the twentieth century."

There was a noble reception in Halifax, quite in
harmony with Mr. Fielding's advance greeting. The
Chamber of Commerce took the visitors in hand for
a sail on the harbour; Hon. Albert Gayton, Minister
of Works and Mines in the Provincial Government,
entertained them to lunch, and the Lieut.-Governor,
Sir Adams Archibald, received them at Government
House. At the luncheon the toasts were coupled with
some names which awaken sleeping memories. A toast
to the Local Government was proposed, we are told,
"in a very humorous speech," by Rev. Mr. Grant,
who in the following October was to accept the Principal-
ship of Queen's University and assume in Ontario a
notable task brilliantly carried out as educationist and
publicist. The "Halifax Press" drew a response from
George Johnson, so well known in after time as Parliamentary reporter and Census Commissioner. Mr.
Fielding likewise spoke, and the toast to "The Ladies"
was fittingly assigned to Mr. J. W. Longley, then chief
editorial writer for the *Recorder*, and in later years the
author of a book on "Love." In New Brunswick, the
Lieut.-Governor, Sir Leonard Tilley, was as courteous
as his Haligonian neighbor, and gave the Association
a luncheon and garden party. Among those foremost

in entertaining the Ontario visitors the eye catches the names of Mayor Fenety, of Fredericton, the veteran journalist, C. H. Lugrin, who was to terminate his newspaper services in distant British Columbia, and William Elder, the great man of the St. John *Telegraph*. The Association, in expressing a number of opinions on various subjects, adopted unanimously the following resolution, which will not be found in the official books of a Registrar of Deeds other than his own:

" This Association desires to acknowledge the efficient services of the President, Mr. C. D. Barr, during his term of office, and to express their warm appreciation of his kindly courtesies and gentllmanly demeanor to the members of the Association during the present annual excursion, as well as to all others with whom he has been brought in contact as our representative."

XVII.

NEWSPAPERS AND PARTY TIES.

At Guelph, on July 9th, 1878, the Association met
with Mr. Innes in the chair. The President dealt
courageously with the relations that ought to exist
between the press and the politicians. He said:

"In another important respect the press of Canada
has made remarkable progress. It has, we may say,
nearly altogether got from under the control of the
politician. We mean by this, that a paper now-a-days
very rarely, and to a very small appreciable extent,
depends for its existence or support on any individual
or party. Parties there will always be, and it is right
that they should be upheld by their own papers. But
they are not now the slaves of the party as we have
seen. The question of 'pap' is now never taken into
account. For the newspaper publisher in Canada it
has happily become an obsolete word. Government
advertising has come to be largely a business arrangement—and it is right that it should be so. It is no
longer looked upon as the means of bolstering up a
weakly sheet, and is scarcely thought of by the publisher in his estimated revenue. The days when
papers looked for their main support to men or Governments have gone by, and instead we have a healthy
business tone among newspaper men, who depend on

the character and excellence of their journals—on enterprise, perseverance, and fair business competition. Scarcely one can now be found who is mean enough to go round hat in hand begging for support, or who will so debase the profession as to play the sycophant to some political magnate for a few dollars. The man who makes his paper worthy of public patronage will in nine cases out of ten not be disappointed in receiving his due share of public support.

"All this infuses a spirit of independence among our newspaper men that is fraught with the best results. Editors are for the most part not afraid now-a-days to talk straight out even at the risk of offending some interested politician. When will the day come when they will do the same even at the risk of impairing party loyalty? The more independent the press becomes, so much the better will it be for parties and the body politic. And the day may yet come—we hope to see it—when all newspapers will be thoroughly and to the fullest extent independent of parties, and when the words and actions of public men will be criticized and judged on their merits alone."

There is nothing in all this inconsistent with the subsequent attitude of the member for South Wellington, who remained to the end of his days one of the kindliest of men and most enlightened of party politicians. A programme of subjects dealing with professional interests had been prepared for this convention. Mr. Barr's advice had borne fruit. The committee had arranged a list of topics calculated to make the most frivolous excursionist quail. Mr. Cameron was to dwell upon the evils of paid matter in the reading columns. Mr. Barr would discuss an advertising rate card. Mr. Creighton was expected to advocate more care in publishing anonymous correspondence. Mr. Trayes was to expound the wisdom of district associations. But lo! What happened? At the last moment the excursionists rallied their cohorts, moved that the promising debates "be allowed to remain over for next year," and the party at once left for Detroit, Chicago, and Milwaukee.

Having been born in Kingston, the Association happily thought of celebrating its twenty-first birthday in its native place with Mr. James Shannon, of the *News*, in the presidential chair. Mr. Shannon referred to the formation of the society in 1859, and to the fact that Dr. Barker, the former publisher of the *British Whig*, still resided in Kingston. The annual address, a clever and scholarly effort, concluded with the announcement that arrangements had been made with the railways for a two cent rate for all *bona fide* members engaged in newspaper work. It appears, therefore, that the railways have successfully maintained this rate for nearly thirty-two years. The excursion was through the Thousand Islands.

In 1880 the annual convention was held in Toronto, and was followed by the third excursion to Lake Superior. In his address President A. Matheson made a fitting allusion to the lamentable death of Hon. George Brown, of *The Globe*.

"During the past year the press of Canada has sustained a severe, perhaps I ought to say an irreparable, loss in the sad and untimely death of Hon. George Brown. Though not a member of this Association, Mr.

Brown was the leading journalist of the Dominion, and it is therefore proper that fitting allusion should here be made to the loss which the press has sustained in his death. Mr. Brown was a statesman, an orator, a leading agriculturist, and an influential and useful citizen, but it was as a journalist that he first made his mark in Canada, and it is the death of the journalist that more deeply affects us. He was undoubtedly a man of great ability, of indomitable courage, of untiring industry and great intellectual power, but it may be safely said that but for the newspaper he conducted, Mr. Brown would never have attained the prominent position he occupied. Like all good journalists, he loved his profession, and he believed in the newspaper as a public educator and as a power to defend the rights and privileges of the people. By his death the press of Canada has lost one of its ablest conductors and most fearless defenders of its freedom."

By passing a formal resolution, the Association had decided to mark in a tangible way the unremitting labours of its secretary, Mr. W. R. Climie, of the Bowmanville *Statesman*. In pursuance of these instructions, the Executive met at the Rossin House, Toronto, November 30th, 1880, and presented Mr. Climie with a handsome silver tea service and an address which contained flattering reference to his zeal and sagacity:

"To you, sir, the Canadian Press Association is mainly indebted for its present prosperity, embracing as it does, in its membership, the leading journalists of the Province of Ontario, who highly value and freely avail themselves of the advantages and privileges which by your untiring labors it has secured to them. Chiefly to you it owes its present exclusively professional character, which at one time it did not possess, and to attain which much weeding out was necessary, a delicate task which could not have been entrusted to more judicious hands than yours. It is also to you that the Association owes the satisfactory condition of its finances. We are aware, further, of the thorough manner in which you have conducted the burdensome correspondence and other business of the office you have held for so many years."

Mr. Climie replied in the modest strain characteristic of all secretaries, and disclaimed having done more than his share of the work, He had been appointed secretary in 1876, succeeding Mr. Buchanan, and continued to act until his retirement in 1890. This is a fitting place to mention these potent functionaries. To the secretary, as is well known, has always fallen the chief burden of administering the affairs of the society, attending to the finances, carrying on the correspondence, and performing the executive duties. As the Association has expanded in membership and activity during the past fifteen years, it has been found convenient to confer this onerous post upon a resident of Toronto, that city being a central point for the transaction of business and for the periodical meetings of the Executive Committee. Mr. J. E. Atkinson was secretary in 1892 and 1893. To him succeeded Mr. J. B. Mac-Lean, whose enterprise in establishing *Canadian Printer and Publisher* as the organ of the Association fulfilled a long-cherished project first mooted by Mr. Josiah Blackburn in 1861. Mr. John A. Cooper was appointed in 1895 and served for seven years with unflagging zeal and intelligence. Mr. J. T. Clark held office for two years and received a valuable token of appreciation for his efforts in carrying out the excursion to the St. Louis Exposition in 1903. In that year Mr. John R. Bone was made assistant secretary, and in 1905 accepted the office to which he has since so loyally devoted himself, discharging at the same time the engrossing tasks of a managing editorship.

President Trayes worthily represented the press as chairman of the banquet to Mr. Goldwin Smith, and his annual address at the Port Hope convention in 1881 showed a thorough grasp of all departments of a newspaper office. Mr. Trayes had served his apprenticeship in the office of the Montreal *Pilot* and, after a short experience in Boston, returned to Canada. In 1864 he founded the Port Hope *Times*. He was chief promoter of the agitation that resulted in the removal of the postage on newspapers, and was one of the deputation which succeeded in having the amendments made in the Ontario libel law, by which newspapers are so much better protected than formerly. He also took a leading part in the work accomplished by the Association in regulating the payment of postage on newspapers. A well-known Mason, he was for many years editor and publisher of the *Canadian Craftsman*.

The Port Hope meeting was followed by an excursion to Peterborough through the lakes of that beautiful district, and then by way of Georgian Bay to Parry Sound, returning to Penetanguishene. During the trip a discussion took place upon the vexed question of postage, which on several occasions since 1859 had been a cause of anguish to Canadian publishers.

XVIII.

HISTORY OF THE ANTI-POSTAGE MOVEMENT.

IT is now in place to give some account of this long-standing controversy. From the hour of its birth the Association had complaints to make of the postal law. At the organization meeting at Kingston in 1859, an agitation was begun to remove the postage charges on newspapers. The grievance is, therefore, as old as the Association itself. There have always been some members of the press who deem the impost a proper one, and who resented the movements for free postage. It is, of course, not necessary to argue the question here. But it is well to look into the history of Canadian newspaper postage in order to show that the postal authorities themselves have not been uniformly in favour of the charges. The Imperial Post Office transferred the Canadian service to the Government of Canada in April, 1851. Up to that date newspaper postage was a perquisite of the chief officer, and the record does not indicate what the rates were.* In 1855 the authorities abolished postage on newspapers mailed from the office of publication. Two years later this privilege was extended to newspapers mailed from

* The former Deputy-Postmaster-General for Canada, Lieut.-Colonel William White, C.M.G., has been good enough to furnish the historical data given here.

Great Britain and France to regular subscribers in Canada. In 1859, however, when Hon. Sydney Smith was Postmaster-General, the authorities reverted to the tax. The charge was one cent a copy on all news-papers sent through the mails, except exchange copies —a perfectly illogical arrangement, since it imposed a tax on the public, but exempted the editors. How-ever, it realized the substantial sum of $50,000. This rate, despite the complaints of the Press Association, remained in force until Confederation, when the other Provinces came in. A new system was then intro-duced. In 1867 each weekly was charged five cents per three months; each semi-weekly, ten cents; each tri-weekly, fifteen cents; each daily, thirty cents. Exchanges were free as before. This anomalous policy lasted until 1875, when a pound rate of one cent to regular subscribers was established. Under the old system the amount of postage was known to each subscriber and he remitted accordingly to the publisher. Under the law of 1875, however, the publishers found it impracticable to collect from the subscriber and thenceforward paid the tax themselves. In 1886, when Sir Alexander Campbell was Postmaster-General, newspaper postage was once more abolished, to be revived by Sir William Mulock in 1898.

The Kingston meeting in 1859 appointed a committee to prepare petitions to Parliament and have publishers generally sign them. The Government showed no disposition to yield until Mr. Foley, the Postmaster-General, assured the deputation from the Association in 1862 that he was personally opposed to the tax, and would urge his colleagues to remove it. In this effort

JAMES SHANNON
President 1878

J. B. TRAYES
President 1880

E. J. B. PENSE
President 1881

GEORGE TYE
President 1882

he failed, and President McDougall in his annual address in 1863 was not slow to express his discontent. "I am free to admit," he said, "that as a supporter of the late Macdonald-Sicotte Government" (this was Sandfield Macdonald, a statesman more addicted to economy and surpluses than his illustrious namesake), "I did feel not a little chagrined when informed that they did not intend to deal with this question of the postage, on the ground that the exhausted state of the exchequer would not admit of their dispensing with the source of revenue it afforded. I may here state, without being considered egotistical, that notwithstanding my strong party leanings—for you will admit that I am sufficiently Grittish for all practical purposes—I did speak out my mind very freely on this subject." The President went on to defend free postage because the people paid the tax, not the publishers, and the readers of newspapers had urged the abolition of the charge. There was also, he added, the fact that the press, like the public school, was a potent means of educating and elevating the masses and was of special value in training men in the duties of citizenship and knowledge of public affairs. These views met with approval, and, on motion of Mr. Mackenzie Bowell, it was resolved to prepare petitions to the "three branches of the Legislature."

At Goderich in August, 1867, President Sellar dealt with postage, and hoped that the new Parliament would carry out for the whole Dominion the policy which had up to that time prevailed in the Maritime Provinces, that of free carriage of newspapers. He quoted from the St. John, N.B. *Telegraph* a strong argument in

7

favour of this course. He pointed out the inconsistency of carrying agricultural and temperance publications free while taxing the rest. A discussion followed. A motion to petition for abolition was adopted. The following year, at Collingwood, President Campbell said:

"The postage question came up for legislation at our first Dominion Parliament when the Postmaster-General (Sir Alexander Campbell) thought proper to impose a high and unreasonable rate upon newspapers. This unjust attempt to impose a tax upon knowledge was warmly and unitedly assailed by the Canadian press without distinction. I felt it my duty to address a circular to the press generally, asking to have that powerful engine use its influence with the members of the different ridings to assail the impost bill. With wonderful promptness and unanimity this appeal was complied with and one obnoxious clause in the Postal Bill was accordingly struck out. It is but justice here to refer to the able and united assistance rendered our efforts in this matter by the editors who have the honour of seats in Parliament. They were prompt and untiring in their opposition to the bill until it was modified to suit their just demands."

When the Association met at Cobourg in 1869, President Buckingham said: "The re-imposition of the petty and vexatious charges on newspapers passing through the Post Office is a notable exception to the general legislation of the time, but it is hoped that as we have been successful during the past year in getting justice done in the matter of postage rates on newspaper correspondence, we will succeed before long in effecting the removal of the post office tax on newspapers themselves." In 1871 President Jackson expressed regret that despite the representations made by the Association during the previous two years, postage was still levied. For several years efforts to change the law ceased. But when the pound rate was imposed in 1875, with prepayment by publishers, President Hough, by general consent, sent a petition to Parliament against the charge. Addressing the Association at the Hamilton meeting in July of that year, he expressed the hope that the new rate might be judiciously employed to enforce subscriptions payable in advance. The Association does not appear to have taken any action on the question for a number of years until in 1881, at the Port Hope meeting, President Trayes suggested that measures be adopted to secure a modification of the law. Petitions were prepared and joint action with the Quebec Association was taken, with the result that President Pense was able to announce in August, 1882, that the requirement of prepayment by publishers had been abolished. Finally free postage was formally proclaimed in 1886.

How the tax came to be revived forms an interesting story. When the Laurier Government was formed in 1896, Mr. Mulock was made Postmaster-General. Wishing to introduce business-like methods into the finances of the Post Office and to make, if possible, revenue meet expenditure, he bethought him of newspaper postage. There had grown up an abuse of the mails by advertising mediums calling themselves newspapers. This had been openly referred to at meetings of the Association. The germ of the movement may be traced to a resolution adopted in 1893, protesting against publications serving as a cloak for guessing and other questionable competitions. In 1895 it was reported that the Government was considering the revival of the postage rate, and several members expressed themselves in favour of such a policy. One or two members, however, advised caution. A report of this interesting discussion will be found in the proceedings of 1895. Then, in 1896, a committee was selected to consider the matter and recommend a change in the regulations so as to rule out illegitimate publications. Next year the division of opinion in the Association on this subject was still more manifest, and in 1897 Mr. Mulock appeared at the annual meeting, and, with frankness and courage, concluded his statement in these words:

"The present condition of affairs cannot be tolerated. I want to proceed, if possible, with the approbation of the Association, but if I cannot get the approbation of the Association, I am going to do my duty." After thorough discussion, the Association, on motion of Mr. P. D. Ross, decided to take no action upon Mr. Mulock's proposals, but favoured a re-arrangement of the tariff on printers' supplies as a condition indispensable to the re-imposition of postage. The revival of the charge came, however, in due course, bearing most heavily on the dailies with large circulations, and though the rates were subsequently reduced, the charges remain to this day.

XIX.

THE FAMOUS EXCURSION TO THE FAR WEST.

FROM this digression into the fruitful field of postage reform, let us return to 1882, when President Pense took the chair at the annual convention at Toronto in August. Mr. Pense dealt effectively with the newspaper topics of the day, and in this respect, to anyone who dips into the records of the past, his address is especially valuable for historical purposes. He pointed to the success of the efforts to have prepayment of postal charges abolished, and to the amendment of the libel law in Ontario, whereby fair reports of public meetings were declared privileged and not ground of action. The return of Messrs. Innes and Somerville to the House of Commons was a matter for congratulation, both gentlemen being past-Presidents of the Association, and noted for their loyalty to its interests. The recent formation of a new press agency in New York for the distribution of news led Mr. Pense to suggest a union of Canadian dailies to utilize the service to the best advantage for the Canadian public. During the year the number of publications in Canada had increased from 565 to 593, of which number 376 were issued in Ontario, and the excursion about to be taken to the new Canadian West would carry the members to a young country already served by a full score of well-printed and well-conducted journals rivalling their Eastern contemporaries in enterprise and progress. The encouraging words of Prince Leopold were quoted as an incentive to higher efforts, this talented son of Queen Victoria having lately declared that "editors are not the representatives of mere private aims and private ambitions, but constitute a body of public functionaries not less important than any of the established departments of the State, being, as it were, the uncovenanted servants of the whole progress and civilization of mankind."

At the conclusion of the meeting, a large party left for Winnipeg and the West by way of Chicago and St. Paul. "The excursion of 1882," says Mr. David Creighton, "is remembered by old-timers as one of the most interesting ever enjoyed by the Association. It was in the days when the contractors for 'Section B' were still wrestling with the rock and muskegs which lie between Lake Superior and the prairie, and the only way of reaching our Province of Manitoba was through the States. The Association, therefore, took the route by way of Chicago, St. Paul, and Minneapolis, from the latter point making delightful side trips to Lake Minnetonka and the Falls of Minnehaha, immortalized by Longfellow. The principal object of the trip was that the editors of the older Provinces might see for themselves the new land of promise which was then attracting attention, and through which rails were being laid over the prairie at a rate which set a pace in railroad building for the world. To that end, from the time they touched Canadian territory they were taken

in charge by the Canadian Pacific Railway, which did
the honours right royally, attaching a supply car to the
train.   Striking Winnipeg in the boom, they were fast
catching the fever, and might have owned the town had
not the proverbial impecuniosity of the profession pre-
vented.   Hearty demonstrations in their honour nearly
painted the towns red at Portage and Brandon, but
to those who know Manitoba of the present day it may
be a surprise to learn that from a short distance west
of the latter town hardly a building was visible from
the train, the only sign of life being the occasional white
tent which showed where an enterprising pioneer was
going to make his home on the prairie.   At that time
where now stands Regina, the capital city of Saskatchewan, was marked by half a dozen tents and not a single
building at Pile-o'-Bones Creek.   The party went on
to the end of the track, and named the station to be
located there Pense, after the President of the year.
Here they all got out and took a hand in railroad building, to the gratification of the navvies, who rested from
their labours while they bossed the job, each member
of the Association driving a spike.   It is to the credit
of the newspaper men that they put the spikes in good
and tight, and though over a quarter of a century has
passed there has never been any trouble from loose rails
at that point.   Here an Indian and squaw with a little
papoose were found on the prairie, and an impromptu
ceremony was got up to name the baby Climie-Pense,
after the Secretary and President, Major Walsh undertaking to see that he would be registered under that
name in the books of the Indian Department.   To
give the ceremony a kind of religious flavour, a collection

was taken up, to the great delight of the Indian and squaw, who understood that part of the proceedings. The Association has long since lost sight of its ward, but no doubt he is still drawing annuities regularly from a grateful country.*

"On the return trip at Broadview, although the little station was the only building there, the Canadian Pacific Railway had liberally spread a table in the wilderness, and under a mammoth tent, brought for the occasion, gave a banquet which still lives in the memories of those who participated in it. Back at Winnipeg a trip was made down the Red River into Lake Winnipeg, and then the party went eastward beyond Rat Portage, where an excursion was taken amongst the beautiful islands of the Lake of the Woods, and then on to the end of the track on Section B, where they saw the marvellous trestlework with which the difficulties of the muskegs were overcome. Here the contractors, Macdonald and Shields, showed what energy can do by spreading another banquet in the wilderness almost rivalling that of the Canadian Pacific Railway at Broadview.

"A little personal incident which will be well remembered furnished great merriment to the party. A young man of Waterloo County, who shall be nameless, wired ahead to Winnipeg to the young lady to whom he was engaged to join the party there and take the trip out West. She duly reported at the train, but the young man, going back into the station for

*Mr. S. Stewart, Chief Clerk of the Department of Indian Affairs, has kindly looked up the record of Mr. Climie Pense, but has been unable to locate this warrior either in the books of the Department or in any newspaper office out West.

something at the last minute, got left. Being amongst strangers, they acted scripturally and took her in, the gallant young gentlemen of the press leaving her no lack of comforting, so that she thoroughly enjoyed the episode, while her disconsolate lover was chasing her over the prairie and did not join her till the second day out. After that, all went merry as a marriage bell, which rung in reality for the pair a short time afterwards. The party returned through the States, as it had gone, and in the after discussions about our marvellous West, many an Ontario and Quebec editor was able to take a more intelligent part for having gone on that trip."

Having gone to one end of the Canadian Pacific Railway track, it was decided to go to the other, so the 1883 convention was taken to Montreal. This was the third meeting in the old city. It marked the quarter century of the Association's existence. President Tye of Brampton was in the chair, and he mentioned briefly some of the principal events in the society's history. He declared that whatever might be said of the organization's influence upon the press of Canada, it had certainly realized all the expectations of its projectors. The state of the Quebec libel law also formed the theme of some remarks in view of the setting aside of a recent plea by the Montreal *Star* that what it had published was true and in the public interest. "No question more concerns the members of this Association," said Mr. Tye, "than the extent of the liability to legal proceedings, for no Canadian judge would venture to charge the jury that 'the greater the truth the greater the libel.' Still, the press should in no case be subject to fine or imprisonment when facts are faithfully stated and free from malicious or injurious comment. It can scarcely be questioned that the public is equally interested in sustaining the liberty of the press in all cases where the interests of the public are manifestly concerned, and also in punishing unwarrantable attacks."

In conclusion he referred to the serious loss Canadian journalism had sustained in the death of the late Hon. Wm. Elder, Provincial Secretary of New Brunswick, and proprietor of the St. John *Telegraph*. Although Mr. Elder was connected exclusively with the journalism and public life of New Brunswick, he deserves to be remembered throughout Canada as a strong advocate of Confederation and national unity. He was a man of culture and scholarship, having been educated in Glasgow and Edinburgh. Intending to become a minister of the Presbyterian Church, he emigrated to St. John and founded the *Colonial Presbyterian*. He finally entered the field of the secular press, and as proprietor and editor of the St. John *Telegraph*, wielded a great influence. He was respected by friend and opponent alike as a man of irreproachable character and a good citizen. He was one of the New Brunswick committee which gave the Association so warm a welcome during its visit to the Maritime Provinces in 1877.

As another twenty-five years have elapsed since the Montreal meeting, it is interesting to read the names of those who attended and were at that date foremost in the work of the press. Amongst the members present in 1883 were:

E. J. B. Pense, *Whig*, Kingston; J. B. Trayes, *Times*, Port Hope; H. Hough, *World*, Cobourg; C. D. Barr,

Post, Lindsay; G. W. Maclean, *World*, Toronto; H. J. Gardiner, *Times*, Hamilton; J. Somerville, M.P., *True Banner*, Dundas; A. J. Matheson, *Expositor*, Perth; W. T. R. Preston, *News*, Port Hope; P. Murray, *Expositor*, Orillia; J. A. Davidson, *Mercury*, Guelph; W. Murray, *Expositor*, Brantford; H. E. Smallpiece, correspondent, *Montreal Journal of Commerce*; M. A. James, *Statesman*, Bowmanville; P. E. W. Moyer, *Daily News*, Berlin; J. Shannon, *Daily News*, Kingston; J. Massie, *Observer*, Cowansville; J. Johnston, *Citizen*, Ottawa; Dr. Clark, hon. member, Toronto; W. E. H. Floyd, *Sentinel-Star*, Newburg; A. Horton, *World*, Toronto; D. Wylie, *Recorder*, Brockville; W. W. 'Cliff, *Central Canadian*, Carleton Place; T. Hilliard, Waterloo; J. Motz, *Berliner*, Berlin; L. and A. Pacaud, *Progrés*, Windsor; J. G. Jackson, *Era*, Newmarket; J. Fullerton, *Review*, Strathroy; J. S. Carman, *Daily Ontario*, Belleville; Rev. E. H. Dewart, D.D., *Christian Guardian*, Toronto; J. E. Davis, *Advocate*, Mitchell; J. J. Crabbe, *Argus*, St. Mary's; J. W. Bengough, *Grip*, Toronto; W. Weld, *Farmers' Advocate*, London; W. Bech, *Peel Banner*, Brampton; W. Butcher, *Telegraph-Herald*, London; T. P. Gorman, Ottawa correspondent, Toronto *Globe;* J. C. Dent, *Monetary Times*, Toronto; J. J. Cave, *Advocate*, Woodville; J. R. Grant, *Post*, Brussels; A. F. Stevenson, *Aurora Borealis*, Aurora; R. Howard, *Star*, Hastings; J. Fullerton, *Canadian Poultry Review*, Strathroy.

There were one hundred in the party, including the ladies, and the Ontario contingent being joined by the members of the Quebec Press Association, visited

Quebec, the Saguenay, Rivière du Loup (where they were addressed by Sir John Macdonald), and had a very pleasant and remarkable excursion. "No one was disappointed," says one member of the party, "and its attractions and enjoyments have been described by many a pen. One incident is recalled during the trip to Lake St. John, north of Quebec, when, on a decidedly hot day, the party took 'buckboards' and their lunches and set out to view the scenery. They became thirsty, and stopping a group of children near a small village, asked for some water. But the youngsters did not seem to understand. Finally, it was discovered that one of the party spoke French fluently. To him all turned with joy. He stepped forward with dignity, made a remark which sounded like this: 'Vooley voo noo dunnay oon vare dough, see voo play?' But a Parisian accent was clearly not understood in that locality. He tried again. At last one of the boys said: 'Oh, fetch it to him in a dipper.' The thirsty ones then drank and enjoyed the joke.

"Sometimes a little romance occurred on these holiday trips. On this occasion a member of the party was a pretty and charming young lady from a small town west of Toronto; also, a handsome and talented young bachelor editor from a prosperous country town further west. It was soon quite apparent that an *affaire du cœur* was in progress. It came to a happy ending when the lamented Andrew Pattullo was engaged to the charming woman who soon after became his wife. Both have passed away.

"To the same excursion party came a somewhat reserved and nice-looking young man from Perth.

He was rather bashful, but he became very popular with the ladies. He was a bachelor. In those days he was better dressed even than he is now, but this is subject to correction. This quiet young editor-lawyer blossomed out into the financial critic of the Opposition in the Ontario Legislature, and in due course into the Treasurer of the Province, and, though he is rolling in wealth from succession duties and surpluses, he is still a bachelor."

XX.

THE MOVEMENT TO REFORM THE LIBEL LAWS.

WHEN President C. Blackett Robinson took the chair at the Toronto convention in 1884, there was present a delegation of Quebec members connected with the French-Canadian journals. This was the natural sequence of the previous year's excursion to Quebec and the cordial hospitality shown to the Ontario visitors by their Quebec friends. The following members of the Quebec Province Press Association are, therefore, given in the list of those registered at the meeting: N. Levasseur, *L'Evenement*, President; Hon. M. de la Bruere, *Le Courrier de St. Hyacinthe;* Thos. Brossoit, *Le Progrès de Valleyfield ;* L. S. Pinault, *L'Electeur;* Jules Tessier, St. John's *Franco-Canadien;* M. and Madame F. E. Roy, *Le Courrier du Canada;* Joseph Tassé, *La Minerve.* Mr. Robinson extended to them a special welcome, and said, "It gives me great pleasure to greet you on this occasion, because such meetings afford an agreeable respite from the ceaseless exacting labours in which we are all engaged." This was the year of the great excursion to the Yellowstone National Park, Wyoming, over the Northern Pacific Railway from Duluth. The journey to Duluth was by rail to Sarnia and through the lakes by the steamer "United Empire."

In 1885 the Association went to New York and Boston, Mr. Erastus Wiman, later on so famous as a pioneer in the cause of Commercial Union, making arrangements for the entertainment of the party with the whole-souled cordiality for which he was noted. Mr. Wiman subsequently plunged into the distracting discussions which shook Canada for several years on the question of our trade policy and secured his full share of the criticism that flew about so generously. But he kept up his friendly interest in the press and philosophically accepted the penalty of his political incursions. He retained to the end of his somewhat unsatisfactory and melancholy career the regard of many Canadian journalists who thought his policy a mistaken one. Before leaving Toronto on this excursion, President George R. Pattullo delivered the annual address. In this he recorded the steady increase in membership and the healthy and permanent vitality that had characterized the Association during the year. The fixed aim of every journalist, he said, was to make his calling better than he found it; to elevate it and to obtain for it full recognition as a permanent and regular profession. The law of libel was still in an imperfect condition and amendments to at least three important points were necessary. Uniformity of the law of libel, as regards prosecutions in civil actions, in all the Provinces of Confederation, was desirable so as to compel a responsible prosecution. The third amendment desirable was in reference to the hardship and injustice imposed upon a journalist in this Province by compelling him to defend an action for criminal libel in another Province. In concluding, Mr. Pattullo made an allusion to the services rendered by the newspaper correspondents with the volunteers in the North West, and expressed the hope that the recent uprising there would, in the end, benefit the country.

The reference to the libel law in the President's address excited some discussion on the subject and the outcome of it was the adoption of the following resolution:

Moved by Mr. J. B. Trayes, seconded by Mr. George Tye:

" That a sub-committee be appointed for the purpose of asking the Ontario and Dominion Governments to make the necessary changes in the libel laws so far as they refer to newspapers; that said committee be empowered to employ counsel and take such further action as may be necessary to secure desirable changes in the law."

The state of the libel law continued for some time to be a subject of agitation. It formed the chief topic of President Davidson's address in 1886. The members were in earnest. Mr. Barr, seconded by Mr. Hough, carried the following resolution:

"That the question of securing desired amendments to the law of libel be remitted to the Executive Committee with a request to hold a special meeting in October, or some convenient date before the next Session of the Ontario Assembly, to invite the attendance thereat of publishers of daily newspapers in Ontario, and such others as they may deem advisable, with the view of fully considering the matter and deciding upon a definite plan of amendment; and that said meeting be requested to

C. BLACKETT ROBINSON
President 1883

G. R. PATTULLO
President 1884

JOHN A. DAVIDSON
President 1885

WM. WATT
President 1886

interview the Attorney-General of Ontario, with the object of securing needed legislation in the premises. The committee was also authorized to secure such legal advice or assistance as they may consider necessary."

The result was an improvement in one or two particulars in the Ontario law, because Sir Oliver Mowat took a somewhat more liberal view of the matter than lawyer-legislators usually do. But the procedure remains cumbrous and expensive to this day, causing enormous cost and needless litigation. The excursion in 1886 was to Chicago by the Lakes.

When the President, Wm. Watt, addressed the annual convention in 1887, the libel law was once more the chief theme of discussion. He congratulated the press of Ontario upon the new law passed by the Legislature. This important measure provided for notice to the publishers specifying the statements complained of, and when a retraction was made, actual damages only could be recovered. Reports of public meetings were privileged. So were accurate reports of court proceedings printed without comment. The publisher could apply for security for costs. Actions must be tried in the county where the chief office of the newspaper was situated or in the county where the plaintiff resided when bringing the action. In view of projected reforms in the federal laws relating to actions for criminal libel, the committee on libel was re-appointed. A vote of thanks was passed to Mr. W. D. Balfour, M.P.P., of the Amherstburg *Echo*, for his exertions in behalf of the Ontario measure. In this vote were included the other editors in the Legislature who had

8

helped to pass it, namely, Messrs. D. Creighton, Owen Sound *Times*, John Carnegie, Peterborough *Review*, and Hon. James Young.   The excursion this year was a trip to Muskoka.

XXI.

A NEW ERA IN ASSOCIATION RECORDS.

WITH 1888 the Association entered upon a new stage of its existence. A journal of proceedings was now established. The annual report, accessible to all members, contains the official record of the work done. The history of the Association since then, therefore, is, comparatively speaking, familiar to most of those now in active service. In order to know what has been accomplished, one has only to consult the reports. It is no longer necessary to delve into fragmentary minute-books; to turn over files of old newspapers; to draw upon the memories of individuals for facts that have become obscured by the cobwebs of time. The past twenty years is the era of business conventions, held during the winter, and primarily based upon the principle of improving the prosperity of the newspaper industry. The competition begotten of many journals issued in a limited field brought on a condition which may fairly be termed acute. The growth of advertising agencies in Canada involved the payment of commissions on advertising. The lowering of subscription rates, in many cases below the profit point, added to the distress. There ensued a time of national commercial depression, never very disastrous, but unrelieved by intervals of trade buoyancy. Under-bidding for printing contracts also sent down prices for printing. The outlook was not encouraging. There were always notable exceptions, both in the daily and weekly fields, to the passion for reducing profits, but, in general, the situation was bad, and the members of the Association, as practical men, realized that something must be done. They knew that a newspaper, to be a power for good, must make money. The price paid for a free, untrammelled press, capable of vigilant public service, is financial independence, and financial independence is born of a certain devotion to the sordid side of things. The sociable element in the Association was admirable, and, as we shall see, it was not neglected. The maintenance of a lofty tone of discussion, and the practice of honourable methods in every branch of the business, which used to form the staple in the addresses to the Association in olden days, continued to be held in the same regard. But not so much was said about them. The lean years seemed to drag along interminably, and the fat years were long in coming.

The duty which now devolved upon the Association was onerous. To keep alive the old social interest; to appeal to the higher motives which inspire the press; and to introduce practical discussions as an impetus to success in business, meant much labour for the executive. From 1888 onward, we find the problem attacked with vigour and courage. The questions then and now of prime importance in the counting room were taken up and concerted action encouraged. If the organization had been conducted as a bank or other corporation conducts its affairs—by sustained effort and a continuous system—some of the issues with which the Association still struggles would have been settled. As a society of voluntary workers with an executive changing from year to year, the progress made was slow, and when a step in advance was recorded, it was not always retained. It is necessary to summarize. From 1888 to 1900 the annual conventions, with the place of meeting and the chairmen, were as follows:

Year.	Place.	President.	Date.
1888	Toronto	Rev. Dr. Dewart	July 31 and Feb. 22, '89.
1889	Toronto	Roy V. Somerville	July 18 and Feb. 14, '90
1890-1	Toronto	Andrew Pattullo	Aug. 5 and Feb. 13, '91
1892	Ottawa	H. P. Moore	March 3–4.
1893	Toronto	A. F. Pirie	Feb. 9–10
1894	Toronto	T. H. Preston	Feb. 9.
1895	Toronto	L. W. Shannon	Jan. 31
1896	Toronto	J. S. Brierley	Feb. 6–7.
1897	Toronto	J. B. MacLean	Feb. 4–5
1898	Toronto	Robert Holmes	March 10–11
1899	Toronto	W. S. Dingman	Feb. 2–3
1900	Toronto	J. S. Willison	Feb. 1–2

At first, as will be observed by the dates, there was a brief summer meeting, a presidential address, and an excursion. All papers and discussions were reserved for a business convention held six months later. This proved too great a strain, and the winter sessions became so popular that, as Aaron's rod swallowed the others, so the winter sessions absorbed all executive efforts, and are now a fixed feature, lasting three days. The programme of subjects during this period of twelve years exhibits great variety. Mr. Roy Somerville, who was to show in the larger fields of Great Britain and the United States a complete grasp of advertising problems, expounded correct methods in weekly publishing. Mr. Pense contributed valuable advice upon the proper equipment for a printing office. The type-casting machine, when first introduced into Canadian offices, was fully described and its economic aspect considered by Mr. P. D. Ross. Mr. Brierley, then in St. Thomas, laid down the sound principles of publishing dailies in small cities. Mr. Erastus Jackson's paper on pioneer journalism in Upper Canada is a fine historical treatise. Mr. Wm. Houston showed how the training of a journalist should be conducted. Mr. John King, more than once, advised the Association in respect to the libel law, and his services were recognized by the presentation of an oil painting of himself from the brush of Mr. Dickson Paterson, R.C.A. Mr. W. S. Dingman dealt with office methods in a thorough manner. Mr. J. F. Mackay, then of Chatham, outlined the work of the subscription canvasser. Machine work, estimating on job printing, advertising, country correspondence, etc., in short, every factor which is essential to the success of daily and weekly newspaper offices, was discussed from year to year with candour, insight, and vigour. The elementary principles of good management were carefully explained by men who knew well what they were talking about. The annual meetings became an actual school of journalism for all those who attended. No theoretical course in a university could have been so thoroughly equipped or could have imparted to its students so effective a system of laboratory training. None of the speakers posed as a superior person gifted with special abilities to lecture others. All were learners, each gave his experience, and received fresh knowledge from contact with his colleagues. Short debates sprang up upon the topics dealt with, and this has led to the illuminating conferences of recent years, when the Association, after holding general meetings, divides itself into sections for the consideration of matters affecting specially one class or another. To employ a favorite expression, the Association found itself during this period, developed a community of interest among the members hitherto not thought of, established friendships on a firmer basis, and made possible co-operation on all the larger questions that affected the profession. When commercial prosperity once more returned, and Canada was swept along the road of national expansion, the newspapers were among the first to profit, and many of the publishers and editors who had contributed so much time and energy to the work of the Association received back in tangible form the fruits of their efforts.

XXII.

PRESIDENTIAL ADDRESSES IN RECENT YEARS.

THE presidential addresses of the period under review must not be passed over. Dr. Dewart, of the *Christian Guardian*, an outstanding figure in the religious press of the country, fittingly referred to the catholic spirit which reigned supreme in the proceedings of the society, where creed and politics were relegated to their proper places. It is interesting, also, to note that he who had never hesitated to avow his political views, strongly recommended to his younger brethren the value of independence in the support given by newspapers to political parties. Only by an exhaustive comparison (made by few) does one realize the gain in this respect during the past twenty years. Mr. Crabbe, who spoke by the book, pleaded for the revival of the printer's art, which had suffered so much from the inroads of machinery and the absence of trained apprentices. Mr. Pattullo, who could with equal facility deliver a brilliant oration upon public affairs or a practical address upon newspaper conditions, contented himself with an effort that appealed to plain men. He warned his hearers against the delusion that the changes in the methods of producing newspapers were all made. "There are many more coming upon us and

no one can predict what the future will bring forth."
Mr. Pattullo was a man of exceptional gifts, and his
devotion to the interests of the press never faltered.
He was elected to the Legislature in 1896, for North
Oxford, and soon attained distinction in that body.
His death in England, during a visit undertaken in
response to an invitation to deliver addresses on questions of Imperial interest, was deeply lamented by his
old friends and colleagues in the Association.

Mr. Moore, who was President in 1893, and worthily
represented the weekly press, aptly defined the status
and purpose of the organization. It had by no means
exhausted its possibilities for usefulness. Although
the aim was distinctly educational, "we can," he said,
"influence legitimate legislation in our interest." The
time was soon to come when Mr. Moore's prediction
would be borne out to the letter. Mr. Pirie, who
occupied the chair in 1894, was one of the wittiest of
speakers and most genial of companions. His talents
won him a high reputation as a writer for metropolitan
journals like the Toronto *Telegram* and the Montreal
Star, and when he purchased the Dundas *Banner* and
settled down to journalism in a country town he gave
a splendid example of what the editorial page in a
weekly paper may be made. His sallies at the annual
banquets and other social gatherings of newspaper
writers were the delight of all who heard them. It
was he who spoke of the danger an editor incurred of
losing "one, if not both, of his subscribers." Looking
blandly about him at a dinner, he expressed the pleasure it gave him to see so many of his *confrères* "wearing
the white shirt of a blameless life." Perhaps his speech

at the banquet in 1895 best illustrates his sparkling humor. He was replying to a toast to "the Press and the Patriots," and defined a patriot as a country editor who prints a paper for $1 a year in cash, or $1.50 in turnips.

"I desire to admit frankly that the members of the country press are not beautiful. But if we are not beautiful, we are good, or, as I told Mr. Willison, of *The Globe*, this afternoon, if we were not good, God would burn down our offices too. (This allusion to the *Globe* fire was received with uproarious laughter.) What is the country press? It is an instrument for keeping people from forming their own opinions. The members of the country press are not suppliants. They are necessary to statesmen. When we get tired of making other people Premiers of this country, we make our own men Premiers. (Sir Mackenzie Bowell was then Prime Minister.) The earth is wobbling on its axis and all this at one dollar a year. Let me do the job printing of this country, and I don't care who makes the laws. Why, only yesterday afternoon, as one of my subscribers was piling up his subscription in my back yard, he said: 'Mr. Pirie, public opinion is at your back.'" The death of this bright and engaging man, in the prime of life, was a great loss to journalism and to the country.

Mr. T. H. Preston's address might have been termed a speech from the throne, so accurately did it reflect the proposals of the time and the outlook before the press of the country. He spoke of the changes involved in the adoption of machine composition; the less rigid adherence of newspapers to party everywhere apparent; the object lesson in fraternal relations presented by *The Globe* staff, after the fire, being hospitably received by Mr. Creighton in the office of their chief political opponent; the appointment of Sir Mackenzie Bowell to the Premiership of Canada, vacant by the lamented death of Sir John Thompson, who had begun as a Parliamentary reporter. Mr. Preston, who was afterwards as a Liberal member of the Legislature to maintain, by his urbanity and dignity in debate, the best traditions of Parliamentary life, made this reference to the new Conservative Premier:

"Sir Mackenzie Bowell, through all his gradations in the public service, has kept in touch with the fourth estate, and I feel satisfied that we, on our part, regardless of political predilections, will congratulate him most heartily, not only on the high office to which long service to the people of Canada entitles him, but on the very deserved honour of knighthood that has been conferred upon him by Her Majesty, the Queen."

Mr. Shannon, who was President in 1896, called attention to the subject of copyright in books, a movement to which, although it conferred no direct advantage upon them, the newspapers, with characteristic generosity, had given a cordial support. Reference was also made to the standing agreement with Mr. John King, K.C., by which editors threatened with law suits could get the benefit of his advice as an authority on the libel law. This arrangement subsequently lapsed, although recent events have proved it to have been a wise provision against unnecessary litigation and threatened blackmail. Mr. J. S. Brierley, the following year, was able to assure the Association that

the newspaper situation was placid, and his address
is remarkable for its correct analysis of two matters
which still await satisfactory settlement: the inequali-
ties of the present postal law, then on the eve of enact-
ment, and the formation of a Dominion Press Association to bring the newspaper interests of all the Provinces
into closer touch. When Mr. J. B. MacLean presided
at the Ottawa convention of 1898, he outlined the basis
for a new cable service which has since developed into
the Canadian Associated Cables. Mr. MacLean also
drew attention to an evil much felt at the time, but
remedied in later years: the accrediting of unsuitable
persons to act in England, at special functions like the
Queen's Jubilee, as correspondents of Canadian papers.
Few complaints of this kind were heard in connection
with the King's Coronation. Another of Mr. Mac-
Lean's suggestions which awaits fulfilment—the appointment of an adequately paid permanent secretary—is as
practical a proposal to-day as it was then. When
Mr. W. S. Dingman took the chair at the forty-first
annual meeting in 1899, he had the satisfaction of
announcing that the paid up membership list had
reached 204, the highest on record, and if anything
were needed to stimulate effort in the work, it would
be found in the eminently fair and encouraging
address of the President, who surveyed the newspaper situation at that date in an intelligent and
thorough manner. He spoke of the great excursion
to the Pacific Coast in 1899, when the members had
had the great opportunity of inspecting the Western
domain with its fertile lands and wonderful scenery.
In 1900, Mr. J. S. Willison omitted the presidential

address, an example first set, it would seem, by
Mr. Bowell, in 1866, for none of the records con-
sulted in that year yields any trace of such a
contribution to the proceedings. But Mr. Willison
repaired this omission by a vigorous speech at the banquet in the evening, when the subject of racial unity
arose out of some remarks by M. Marc Sauvalle, of
La Presse. This brilliant French-Canadian declared
(what no one will accept) that he spoke English badly,
and perhaps some of his hearers, he said, spoke French
imperfectly. "But," he went on, "there is a language
which everybody can understand, that is the language
of goodwill and loyalty—all for all and each for the
other. The more the two races meet, the more interest
there will be between us." With characteristic alert-
ness, Mr. Willison seized the opportunity to urge the
making of loyalty to Canada as the first and best test
of Canadian citizenship. He was not going to assess
the measure of responsibility (Mr. Willison is reported
as saying) for the use of the wholly mischievous and
unnecessary race and creed cries. He hoped that
before many years there would be an end to them. It
was impossible for us as a people to give proper attention to the great financial and economical problems
which claimed solution until we got rid of these mischievous, these infernal topics. He put the responsibility for these unhappy discussions upon the press
and the politicians, not upon the public. Appeals of
that nature never came up from the people; they came
down from the politicians. He was bound to say, too,
that too often the corruption they all deplored came
from the top rather than from the bottom. It was not

always the Canadian elector who wished to sell his vote. It was too often the politician who wished to buy it. The Canadian press should do a great deal more than it ever had to put down these practices, and give more decency and dignity to public life.

The ring of manly courage and independence in these utterances is worthy of the high reputation of the speaker, and it is due to the Association to say that its official spokesmen, from 1859 down to the annual address of President McNee in 1905, have never shown the crouching spirit, but have vindicated freedom of opinion and liberty of speech as the foundation stone of journalism.

XXIII.

THE GREAT COMBAT WITH THE PAPER COMBINE.

DURING the past seven years the record of the organization may be briefly summarized. The Presidency of Mr. A. G. F. Macdonald was signalized by a successful excursion to the Maritime Provinces, rivalling that of 1877. The Presidential terms of Mr. McGillicuddy, Mr. Pettypiece, and Mr. Cooper saw the culmination and results of the famous fight with the Papermakers' Association, while Mr. McNee in 1905 had the satisfaction of welcoming the members of the Eastern Townships Press Association, that body having affiliated with the parent society under its President, Mr. L. S. Channell, of Sherbrooke. But all the events of this period are dwarfed in importance by the combat with the paper combine. Scarcely any incident in the past fifty years exhibits in so remarkable a manner the value of a mutual understanding and co-operation. The Association had been in effect, although not in name, an Ontario organization. But on this occasion all the principal publishers in Canada, from Halifax to Victoria, joined in the common effort to resist what was honestly felt to be an illegal exaction striking at the root of newspaper prosperity. The Canadian Press Association, being the largest and oldest body of its kind, managed the plan of campaign from first to last, being supported by expressions of confidence from the other associations and from publishers all over Canada. Where so many rendered valuable advice and assistance, it is difficult to single out individuals, but the prime movers in the fight were Messrs. J. A. Cooper, J. E. Atkinson, P. D. Ross, T. H. Preston, M.P.P., D. McGillicuddy, and H. J. Pettypiece, M.P.P. When the delegation from the Association appeared before the Dominion Government at Ottawa, asking for a Royal Commission, as provided for in such cases by the Tariff Act, they were supported by Senator Templeman, Hon. J. I. Tarte and other journalistic members of Parliament.

The cause of this spirited contest, needless to say, was an alarming rise in the cost of paper, and in this connection it is instructive to review the course of prices. In 1899 the larger dailies were buying paper all the way from $1.70 to $2.10 per hundred; the cash discount was four to five per cent., and the credit period was four months. Early in February, 1900, the Ottawa *Journal* was offered a new contract at $2.23. Immediately after the adoption of the papermakers' agreement on February 21st, 1900, the price of rolls advanced to $2.50, and reams to $2.75. The Chatham *Planet* had been paying $2.10 for reams and were asked $2.75 on the renewal of a contract which existed about this time. When the Eddy mills were burned in April, 1900, the publishers tried to get paper from the International Paper Company, of New York, but were referred to Canadian makers, thus showing that there was a compact between the two associations not

J. J. CRABBE
President 1887

E. H. DEWART. D.D.
President 1888

ROY V. SOMERVILLE
President 1889

ANDREW PATTULLO
President 1890

to enter each other's territory. This was the situation which forced the Press Association to take action. In May, 1900, the Executive, by a resolution, condemned the increase in the price of paper which resulted from the formation of the Papermakers' Association a few months previously. At the annual meeting in March, 1901, the Association went farther and demanded an investigation at the hands of the Dominion Government. On April 10th, a deputation of publishers visited Ottawa and laid their case before Mr. Fielding and Mr. Paterson, asking them to act at once upon the anti-combine clause of the Tariff Act (Sec. 18: Chap. 16, 60 and 61 V). This demand was embodied in a formal document couched in the following terms:—

THE CANADIAN PRESS ASSOCIATION,
                    TORONTO, *April 10th*, 1901.

Honourable W. S. Fielding, Minister of Finance,
    Ottawa:

HONOURABLE SIR:—On May 18, 1900, the Canadian Press Association, at a meeting in Toronto, discussed for the first time the Papermakers' Association and the effects of that Association upon the public interests At that time the following resolution was passed:—

"That the Executive of the C.P.A. believe that a combine now exists among Canadian Paper Manufacturers, the effect of which is to unduly increase the price of news and printing paper, contrary to Section 18 of the Customs Tariff Act of 1897. That this Executive is prepared to submit witnesses and evidence in support of this statement, and we, therefore, respectfully ask that the

9

Government order an investigation under Section 18 and sub-sections of the Customs Tariff Act of 1897, with a view of ameliorating the existing condition."

At the annual meeting of the Press Association, this resolution was reaffirmed, and is now submitted to you for the consideration of yourself and the Government.

We have, etc., A. G. F. McDONALD,
President.

(Sgd.) JOHN A. COOPER,
Secretary-Treasurer.

As no previous action had ever been taken under this clause, the application of the press excited much attention in Parliamentary circles. Further, if the request of the Association was met, what would be the method of procedure and who would pay the bills? The latter point was the one which caused most trouble. At first Mr. Fielding declined to pay more than the fees of the judge and a stenographer. As for counsel and witness fees, these were to be left to the parties themselves. The Press Association objected to being saddled with the expense of prosecution, claiming that it was a matter of public policy. It was only after a blank refusal to appear before the Commission at all, that Mr. Fielding yielded the point in regard to witness fees. The Association in the end was compelled to pay all other expenses, which amounted to about $1,700.

The Order-in-Council authorizing the investigation was dated April 25th. It commissioned Mr. Justice

Taschereau, of the Superior Court of Quebec, to investigate the case. He held sessions in Montreal, Toronto, and New York, where publishers and papermakers appeared before him and stated the two sides of the case. The first sitting was held July 30th and 31st, when Mr. Aylesworth summed up the case for the newspapers, and Mr. W. J. White made the papermakers' defence. On November 27th, the judge sent in his report,* and the finding was in favour of the Press Association. The judge decided that there was a combine, and that it had unduly advanced prices. Twelve papermakers had paid in $500 to this combine and had signed a most uncompromising agreement. That the prices were high and that the Press Association was right in its contention was further proved by the action of the Papermakers' Association on May 10th, just fifteen days after the appointment of the Royal Commission. The price of paper was then voluntarily reduced from $2.50 to $2.37½ for rolls, and from $2.75 to $2.62½ for sheets. The period of credit, which had been reduced from four to three months, remained the same, however, though the new regulations as to freight rates were considerably modified. These changes were important, and amply justified the publishers for the trouble and money which were required to plan and carry on the notable struggle against a formidable group of manufacturers. If the action taken by the Government was not as drastic as some expected, it constituted on the whole a signal vindication of the movement. The duty on news print was reduced from twenty-five per cent. to fifteen per

*See Can. Sess. Papers, No. 53, 1902.

cent, when imported in large quantities, and this action taught a lesson to the paper manufacturers which has not been without permanent effect.

In the foregoing sketch of the Canadian Press Association there are defects and omissions of which the writer is only too conscious. No adequate attempt has been made to connect the record of the society with the general history of the press of Canada. So ambitious an undertaking is left to a worthier pen. Yet with that history the Association is closely interwoven. In no other portion of the English-speaking world has the rise of the press to authority and influence in the State been more conspicuous than in Canada. It has served the country well; it has contributed greatly to the consolidation of the Dominion; it has been foremost in moulding public opinion and in disseminating information. The Association founded in 1859 has been no inconsiderable factor in this work. It contributed men of light and leading to public life. Its members at no time made large claims of superiority, nor did they assert an exclusive right to speak for the press. But they kept alive the spirit of amity, toleration, and national optimism through many a trying ordeal, and no active journalist can examine the half century of achievement without a glow of pride that the best traditions of his profession have been so staunchly maintained by the body which now celebrates its jubilee under the auspices of President J. T. Clark.

A. H. U. Colquhoun.

IN THE MARITIME PROVINCES

IN the Dominion the light of the morning sun and of the evening stars first falls upon the Atlantic coast. It was thus also with the light that radiates from the printing office and the newspaper press. To the fair city of Halifax belongs the honor of these first things in the intellectual life of Canada. It was there the pioneer press was set up and there the first newspaper of our common country was given to the reading public.

Mr. E. B. Biggar in his interesting and valuable "Sketch of Canadian Journalism," contributed to the Canadian Newspaper Directory of 1902, has given particulars of this first newspaper together with a *fac simile* of its pages. It is a modest sheet of two pages, about nine by fifteen inches in size, and was called the Halifax *Gazette*, and issued in 1752. The imprint tells that it was "Printed by John Bushell at the Printing Office, Grafton Street, where advertisements are taken in."

Two other *Gazettes* marked the beginning of newspaper life in New Brunswick and Prince Edward Island respectively, but at a much later date. The first of these was the *Royal St. John's Gazette* and Nova Scotia *Intelligencer*, issued in St. John, December, 1783, and the other was the *Royal Gazette*, first published in

Charlottetown in 1791. All these early *Gazettes* were official organs and contained the governmental notices and announcements of the time along with a modicum of the news of the world, most of it painfully old at the time of its appearance.

Behind the Halifax *Gazette* was a bit of history which carries us back to the first printing press and the first newspaper in America. For John Bushell printed the Halifax paper on a press brought thither by Bartholomew Green the younger, who was a son of Bartholomew Green who printed the first numbers of the Boston *News Letter*, the first American newspaper, and he in turn was son of Samuel Green, the recognized pioneer of printing on the American continent. The younger Green died a month after his arrival in Halifax, and thereupon John Bushell, a former partner of his in the printing business in Boston, came on and, with some financial assistance from Hon. Otis Little, the Attorney-General, began the publication of the *Gazette* the following spring. The first issue bears date March 23, 1752.

This was the year after the adoption of "New Style" in the calendar throughout the British dominions, and the *Gazette* recorded the fact under date of London, September 18, 1751.

John Bushell retained control of the *Gazette* till 1760, and in that year took Anthony Henry into partnership, and soon afterward died. Henry succeeded to the business, but soon got into trouble with his official patrons, who in 1776 brought another printer, one Robert Fletcher, from London with his plant, and he on August 14 of that year sent out the Nova Scotia

Gazette. This was a full sheet of crown folio and was issued weekly at a subscription price of twelve shillings. "Advertisements of moderate length" were inserted at "three shillings each."

In the meantime Henry was not idle; he continued his job printing, and in January, 1769, brought out a small eight-page paper called the Nova Scotia *Chronicle and Weekly Gazette* at a subscription price of eight shillings. The new paper was the first to give attention to local news, and succeeded in awakening public interest. As Henry prospered he bought back the Halifax *Gazette* in 1770 and incorporated it with his own under the name of the Nova Scotia *Gazette and Weekly Chronicle*, and held the post of King's Printer for forty years until his death. His godson, Anthony Henry Holland, became, in 1813, the founder of the *Acadian Recorder*, which still lives and prospers, the oldest newspaper in the Maritime Provinces.

But we must go back to the Boston *News Letter* again for a bit of history of more than passing interest. It had been maintained by Mrs. Draper, after the death of her husband, as a staunch British journal down to the time when Boston was evacuated, upon which event she gathered up her presses and type and came to Halifax, bringing with her John Howe, the father of Joseph Howe, who was long after to fill so large a place in the journalism, statesmanship, and history of the Maritime Provinces and of Canada.

On the way to Halifax John Howe married Miss Minus, a girl of seventeen years, and in January, 1781, he founded the Halifax *Journal*, which was destined to a continuous existence of ninety years. He himself lived to the good old age of eighty. In the meantime William Minus, brother of Mrs. Howe, who also came to Halifax a mere boy with the Loyalists, graduated from his brother-in-law's office and established the *Weekly Chronicle*.

In what is now New Brunswick, but was still a part of Nova Scotia and then known as the County of Sunbury, the St. John's *Gazette* and Nova Scotia *Intelligencer* was established in St. John in December, 1783, and was published by Lewis and Ryan, which name was changed in the following year to the New Brunswick *Gazette and General Advertiser*. In 1785, *The Royal Gazette and Weekly Advertiser* succeeded the aforementioned journals and was published by Christopher Sower, the first King's Printer of the new province. Sower was born in Pennsylvania and brought up to the printing business. He adhered to the British side in the revolutionary troubles, and in consequence his large property was confiscated. After the close of the war he went to London and was rewarded for his loyalty by being made King's Printer and given a colonel's commission. He built for himself a large two-storey house of logs at Hammond River, some fifteen miles from St. John, to serve both as an office and a dwelling, and there the official *Gazette* and the journals of the Legislature were printed and all the official printing was done. Caleb McCready, a great-grand-uncle of the writer of this article, married a daughter of Sower. The latter died in Philadelphia, whither he had gone on a business trip.

The beginning of newspapers in Prince Edward Island, as already stated, was the publication of the

Royal Gazette, first issued in 1791, at Charlottetown. The Island was then a separate province, and for eighteen years previous had enjoyed the distinction of having a Government and Legislature of its own. The community was small and the conditions primitive. The population of the province did not exceed four thousand souls.

The first regular newspaper, apart from the merely official organ, came more than thirty years later, and was established by James D. Haszard in 1823. He was the son of a Loyalist, whose father had proved his devotion to his sovereign by refusing to receive back his confiscated property at the price of becoming a citizen of the new republic. Mr. Haszard is also gratefully remembered as the benefactor of many whom he aided during the "famine" of 1837, and also for having established the first carding and cloth-dressing factory in the province. Mr. Haszard's paper was called the Prince Edward Island *Register*, and in its first issue made a trenchant exposure of some high-handed acts of Governor Smith and some of his near relatives. The result of this was that he was at once cited to appear in the Court of Chancery, of which the Governor himself was Chancellor. He was permitted to make a brief statement of his defence, when the Chancellor addressed him: "I compassionate your youth and inexperience. Did I not do so, I would lay you by the heels long enough to remember it. You have delivered your evidence fairly, clearly, and as becomes a man. I caution you when you publish anything again, keep clear, sir, of a Chancellor. Beware, sir, of the Chancellor!"

The first half of the nineteenth century in the Maritime Provinces was a time of pioneers living in log huts, battling with the forest; of making roads to widely separated settlements; a time of mounted evangelists, riding along bridle paths to fervidly proclaim the Gospel as they understood it; a time of New Light revivals that swept thousands into the Baptist and Methodist churches, which were not churches at all to the ruling classes of Churchmen; a time when Catholic emancipation had yet to be won in the colonies after it had been won in Britain; a time when Baptist and Methodist ministers were put in jail if they dared to solemnize marriage between the members of their flocks; a time when a Dissenter or a Roman Catholic could not hold the office of justice of the peace or constable; a time of Family Compacts ruling by a claim of divine right over peoples whom they held in close subjection.

But the time soon came that saw these masses moving from beneath, with a giant's strength, to "make and break and work their will," and all these shackles and impediments to freedom were one by one swept away. It was under circumstances such as these that Joseph Howe launched the *Nova Scotian* newspaper in Halifax; attacked the irresponsible magistracy that ruled there, was arrested for libel, pleaded his own cause and won it, and was carried home in triumph on the shoulders of a rejoicing people. And as he fought on, an unwearied soldier of the press and of the tribune, to win equal rights, responsible government, and the abolition of class privileges, his newspaper office became a "school of the prophets" of reform and progress.

George E. Fenety learned the printing business in Howe's office and imbibed much of his courage and liberty-loving spirit, and crossing to St. John launched the *Morning News* in 1839, as a champion of popular rights—the first penny paper printed in America. He had none of Howe's speaking power, but he was a hard worker, knew something of the value of news, and was a very capable business man. His paper grew in influence, prospered, and became a powerful factor in promoting like reforms to those which Howe and his associates were urging forward in Nova Scotia.

Edward Whelan, a poor Irish boy whom Howe had taken to his heart and home, learned the printing art in the *Nova Scotian* office, went to Charlottetown and there established first *The Palladium* and a few years later *The Examiner*, under a motto from Euripides, which it still carries—"This is True Liberty when Freeborn Men Having to Advise the Public May Speak Free." He fought a sturdy battle for equal rights, responsible government, for the rights of the Island tenantry, and for free schools, down to the date when these were gained, and later became the eloquent advocate of the union of the provinces. He died in the year 1867, when four provinces had been joined together, while his own province was still remaining without the fold.

David Howe, an elder brother of Joseph Howe, was for some years editor of the St. Andrew's *Herald*, established at St. Andrew's, N.B. Thus closely was the journalism of the three provinces connected in its personnel and in spirit. There were other journals of the pioneer period that ought to be mentioned, notably the New Brunswick *Courier*, established by Henry Chubb in 1811, the best newspaper of its time in the province down to the establishment of the *Morning News*, and the first to become a paying property. The *New Brunswicker*, published in St. John by Till Brothers, is also still favorably remembered by readers of the older generation.

Timothy Warren Anglin came from Ireland to St. John, and about 1854 established *The Freeman*, which he conducted with much ability for many years, and which figured conspicuously in the public discussions from that date down to near the close of the century. John V. Ellis went to St. John from Halifax and with a partner planted *The Globe*, which still flourishes and has always possessed a peculiar charm for a large reading circle. *The Globe*, along with Mr. Anglin's *Freeman*, were opponents of the scheme of confederation.

John Livingston went from Richibucto to St. John, and after some time engaged on the *Morning News* under Mr. Fenety, started *The Telegraph* in 1862. He was a genial man, a trenchant campaign writer, and pushed his paper rapidly to the front. A little later Rev. William Elder established the *Morning Journal*, both this and *The Telegraph* being tri-weeklies and published on alternate days. In process of time, the two papers were united and as a daily attained still wider influence and popularity under the management of Mr. Elder, till it stood in the front rank of Maritime newspapers. Shortly after Mr. Elder's death in 1883, the writer of this article succeeded to the editorial charge of *The Telegraph*, which he held for nearly ten years, when, on a change of the proprietorship, he was in turn succeeded by Dr. Hannay, the historian of Acadia. After several later changes, about five years ago E. W. McCready, A.M., only son of the former editor of the same name, was called to the editorial chair of *The Telegraph*, which position he still retains.

It was the golden age of New Brunswick journalism when William Elder, John Livingston, John V. Ellis, and T. W. Anglin were the leading editorial writers in St. John with a number of bright young men engaged under them. The *Daily Sun* was established in 1877, and has been a strong newspaper from its inception, principally under the successive editorial direction of John Livingston and S. D. Scott, the latter being its editor from 1885 down to the change in ownership about a year ago. Halifax also possessed a galaxy of bright newspaper men about the time of the union of the provinces, including the Annands, William and Charles, who succeeded in line to Joseph Howe's *Nova Scotian* (now *The Chronicle*), and under whom W. S. Fielding developed his abilities as an able and luminous public writer; the Blackadars of the *Recorder;* Compton, of *The Express;* J. C. Crosskill and J. G. Bourinot on *The Reporter;* E. M. McDonald, George Johnson, Martin J. Griffin, and others whose names will quickly recur to the memory of the yet living newspaper readers of that time. The Halifax *Herald*, established in 1878, grew to be a power under the management of the late J. J. Stewart.

In Prince Edward Island a number of vigorous newspapers, not all of them destined to long life, bridged the time between Haszard's *Register* and Whelan's

Examiner. Among these were *The Islander*, established by the late John Ings in 1842, and continued for thirty years; Ross's *Weekly* from 1859 to 1866; *The Island Argus*, founded and conducted by James H. Fletcher in 1869 and continued till 1881, when it was absorbed into *The Examiner.* In 1864 *The Patriot* was established by David Laird as a weekly, becoming a daily in 1882. It was a forceful Liberal journal under Mr. Laird, and when he took office in 1874, under the late Henry Lawson. Mr. Laird resumed its management after his retirement to private life and remained its editor down to 1896, since which time it has been creditably conducted by Frederic J. Nash. The three daily newspapers of Prince Edward Island at the present time are *The Guardian*, independent in politics, and the only morning daily issued in the province, which for the past twelve years has been under the editorial charge of the writer of this article; *The Patriot*, last above referred to, and *The Examiner*, a Conservative journal, of which W. L. Cotton has been editor and proprietor for a lengthened period.

In this brief sketch only the metropolitan newspapers of the three provinces have been referred to and space will not permit mention of the host of journals that have sprung up outside of Halifax, St. John, and Charlottetown, some of them, notably the dailies of Moncton and Sydney, of very vigorous growth and conducted with ability. The three original *Gazettes* which marked the beginning of newspaper life in the Maritime section of Canada have multiplied to twenty-two daily papers and more than a hundred weeklies and semi-weeklies, which minister to the reading public of every city, town, and larger village. It may be mentioned that the Maritime newspapers have from a very early day been owned and controlled almost entirely by men bred on Maritime soil. They have very rarely imported a man from the west. J. T. Hawke, the prosperous editor and proprietor of *The Transcript*, of Moncton, is almost the only example of a western newspaper man who has come eastward. But from Eastern Canada not a few have gone, from time to time, to the west. Among these were Martin J. Griffin, who went from a Halifax newspaper to *The Mail*, of Toronto, and is now Parliamentary Librarian at Ottawa. John Livingston, of St. John, was in later years editor of the Montreal *Herald*, the *Empire*, of Toronto, and the *Herald*, of Calgary, successively. Amor deCosmos, founder of the Victoria, B.C., *Colonist*, was a Nova Scotian, while a later editor of the same journal was C. H. Lugrin, a New Brunswicker and at one time editor of the St. John *Telegraph*; still later Henry Lawson, formerly editor of *The Patriot*, of Charlottetown, filled the editorial chair of *The Colonist* for some time down to his death. Thomas Gorman, some time editor of the *Free Press*, Ottawa, was a graduate from a Prince Edward Island newspaper office, as was also J. K. McInnis, of the Regina *Standard*, and many other names might be mentioned in the same connection, or of the still larger number who have made names for themselves in connection with newspapers in the United States.

The people of the Maritime Provinces are a reading people and support their favorite newspapers loyally. It has been claimed with some show of plausibility that in the smaller field down by the sea may be found the newspaper having the largest circulation in proportion to the population of the city and province in which it is issued. Be that as it may, and while the weight of the larger and more widely circulated journals of the big central provinces is a greater factor in moulding the public opinion of the Dominion, the people of the east are not unreasonably proud of their best newspapers and of the able and patriotic public writers who during a century past championed the cause of reform, and led the way in the march of intellectual, political, and material advancement.

Quite a number of the Maritime journalists were from time to time elected to the provincial Legislatures or the Canadian Parliament, or both in succession. Among these were Hon. Joseph Howe, who served for years in the Legislature and Government of his province, and afterwards as a member of the House of Commons and Secretary of State, and died in office as Lieutenant-Governor of his native province. E. M. McDonald, of the Halifax *Citizen*, was elected to the first Canadian Parliament as representative of the county of Lunenburg. Hon. W. S. Fielding, for twelve years past Minister of Finance at Ottawa, was for many years editor of *The Chronicle* at Halifax, and was also for a long term Premier of Nova Scotia. Hon. Timothy Warren Anglin was repeatedly elected a member of the House of Assembly of New Brunswick; was for a time a member of the Provincial Government, and also served in the first two Parliaments of the Dominion, becoming Speaker under the Mackenzie Administration in 1874. Hon. Edward Willis, of the

St. John *Morning News*, served in the New Brunswick Legislature. Hon. William Elder was for some time Provincial Secretary of New Brunswick, and died in office in 1883. Hon. John V. Ellis, the veteran editor of the St. John *Globe*, had seen service in the Provincial Legislature and in the House of Commons before his appointment to the Senate of Canada. Hon. David Laird, of the Charlottetown *Patriot*, served with distinction in the Island Legislature and later in the House of Commons, and as Minister of the Interior, and is now Indian Commissioner in Winnipeg. Of those here named, only Mr. Fielding, Mr. Laird, and Senator Ellis are now living.

J. E. B. McCready.

IN THE PROVINCE OF QUEBEC,
1858-1908.

HOW marked and significant is the contrast between the newspaper press of the Province of Quebec as it is to-day and the press of the same Province fifty years ago, only those who have some recollection of that far-off time can even imagine. If it be asked in which section of our population the contrast is the more striking and inevitable, the answer may be given without hesitation. The dingy offices in which French-Canadian editors whose names have long been historic were willing to write their appeals to reason or to sentiment would excite unconcealed distaste in their more fastidious successors of the twentieth century. This is but one point of contrast, but it means much. It suggests a progress so comprehensive that it was absolutely undreamed-of in the days that form the starting-point of this hurried retrospect. Nevertheless, before the summer of 1858 was quite completed, an event had occurred which, though it was followed by catastrophe, prompted to the thoughtful mind endless possibilities of development for the press of Canada, as for that of the world at large. The writer can well recall the illuminations and other signs of rejoicing with which Montreal greeted the short-lived triumph of the first Atlantic cable. The words of peace and friendship that passed between Queen Victoria and President Buchanan were, alas! to have for sequel the awful strife of the Civil War before the failure of 1858 was succeeded by a fruition that had "nulla vestigia retrorsum." But the great fact had been accomplished, and men like the late Lord Kelvin (then Professor Thomson, F.R.S.) knew that no casualty could do worse than postpone the operation of oceanic cables. How much the growth of the Canada of our Association's birth and infancy into the Canada of 1908 has been due to the influence of the telegraph, it is needless to insist. That force which stands for the grandest achievement of our time had its culminating moment in that victory of August, 1858. The All-Red Route was still far off, but in the forecast of science and faith it was assured.

Our point of departure (1858), while to us it suggests the day of small things, was regarded very differently by the Canadian contemporaries of Cyrus Field and his co-workers. Two years earlier, in the fall of 1856, took place what is still remembered in Montreal as the Grand Trunk Celebration. Three years earlier the Boston Jubilee had brought together the chief men of standing and influence in both countries—including the President of the one and the Governor-General of the other. Six years after the birth of our Association, the hundredth anniversary of journalism in central Canada was commemorated at Quebec by the representatives of William Brown and Thomas Gilmore.

In the Province of Quebec (which originally included what is now known as Ontario), the establishment of journalism was one of the immediate results of the transfer of Canada to Great Britain. On the 21st of June, 1764, only five years after the arrival of Wolfe at Quebec, the leading inhabitants of the capital beheld the novel sight of a newspaper printed within their own walls, and containing local news and advertisements. William Smith, in his History of Canada, credits Messrs. Brown and Gilmore with the introduction, not only of journalism, but of the art of printing. M. Phileas Gagnon, in his *Essai de Bibliographie Canadienne*, says that Bishop de Pontbriant had a press for printing his mandements. M. Gagnon's statement deserves serious attention. It must be borne in mind that journalism had been in operation in Halifax for seven years before Messrs. Brown and Gilmore reached Quebec. What interests us especially, however, in connection with this pioneer newspaper is that it lived to celebrate its hundredth anniversary. On the 21st of June, 1864, Mr. Middleton, the actual proprietor, issued a centennial number, including a fac-simile of the first *Gazette*. Mr. Middleton became its owner and conductor on the death in 1848 of Hon. John Neilson, a nephew of William Brown, of the original firm. The story of our earliest Quebec newspaper is thus brought within the scope of the present volume. Fourteen years after the foundation of the Quebec *Gazette*, Montreal thought well to follow the example. The story of Fleury Mesplet, who founded *La Gazette Litteraire* of Montreal in 1778, has been told with admirable fullness by Mr. R. W. McLachlan, in a paper read before the Royal Society of Canada in May, 1906. According to Dr. Dionne, seven newspapers, printed at least partly in English, had been founded in the Province of Quebec before the close of the eighteenth century. In 1805 the Quebec *Mercury* was founded by the head of the Cary family, in whose possession it remained for nearly a century. The *Mercury* closed an eventful career on the 17th of October, 1903.

On October 19, 1811, appeared the first number of the Montreal *Herald*. Its first proprietor was William Gray; its first editor, Mr. Mungo Kay, who died in September, 1818. In June, 1823, N. Mower, however, began the publication of the *Canadian Magazine and Literary Repository*. It was conducted by Joseph Nickless, and made its appearance once a month. Four bulky volumes of nearly six hundred pages each bear witness to the enterprise of the publishers and to the aspirations of the contributors. Newton Bosworth says the magazine was well edited and that some of its contents were of a high order of merit. But it failed to receive the support that it deserved. Almost contemporary with the *Canadian Magazine* was the *Canadian Review and Literary and Historical Journal*, which was published quarterly from July, 1824, until September, 1826, forming five numbers of about two hundred and forty pages each. Some years later the *Literary Garland* was undertaken by Mr. John Lovell, and edited by Mr. J. Gibson, assisted latterly by Mrs. Cushing. It was a monthly magazine of tales, sketches, poetry, and music. The first series lasted from 1838 to 1842; the second, from 1843 to 1852. Among the contributors to the *Literary Garland* were Dr. William Dunlop, Mrs. Leprohon (Miss Mullin), Mr. Andrew Robertson, Mr. Fennings Taylor, Mrs. (Col.) McLachlan, Mr. Hugh G. Montgomery. The Montreal *Wit-*

ness was founded on the 5th of January, 1846, as a weekly paper. In August, 1860, it was made a daily, and, under the control of the late Mr. John Dougall, became a journal of widespread influence, especially in the cause of temperance. The Quebec *Morning Chronicle* was established in May, 1847. In January, 1854, it entered definitely into the ranks of the daily press and has ever since exerted a large political and social influence. Among its editors have been Charles Roger, Isaac Watson, George Stewart, E. T. D. Chambers, and J. J. Proctor, who has charge of it at present. The *Pilot*, founded by Sir Francis Hincks, in May, 1844, was for some years a journal of considerable importance. For a time the founder edited it himself. It then (1848) passed under the control of Mr. William Bristow, who, on starting the *Argus* in 1854, left the *Pilot* in charge of Dr. J. P. Litchfield. The *Transcript*, started in 1834, by Donald McDonnell, was edited first by Robert Abraham, and after the *Argus* had ceased to exist, by William Bristow. In its last years A. N. Rennie had charge of it. In 1867 it passed into the hands of Mr. John Lovell, who re-named it the *Daily News*. In May, 1857, a newspaper named the *New Era* was founded by (the Hon.) Thomas Darcy McGee, who had recently removed from the United States to Canada. A few months later Samuel James Watson started the *Irishman*. Both these journals were bright and vigorous. But to-day they are almost forgotten.

The earliest paper published in the Eastern Townships was the *Farmers' and Mechanics' Journal and Eastern Townships Gazette*, which was founded by

Messrs. Walton and Gaylord at Sherbrooke, in 1834. In 1838 it became known as the Sherbrooke *Gazette*, but remained under the same proprietors until 1870, when Messrs. Walton and Gaylord sold it to Messrs. Bradford and Morehouse. The Stanstead *Journal* was founded in 1845 and was for some time conducted by Mr. L. R. Robinson. It is issued at present by the Stanstead Journal Company. The St. John *News and Frontier Advocate* was founded in 1848 by Mr. E. R. Smith and has maintained its well-earned character and circulation for sixty years. A paper known at first as the *Advertiser and Eastern Townships Sentinel* was founded at Knowlton in January, 1856, with the support of Hon. Messrs. Knowlton, Huntington and Moore, and Mr. H. S. Foster. In the following year it became the Waterloo *Advertiser*, and is now owned and controlled by Mr. C. H. Parmelee, M.P. Another ably conducted paper is the *Canadian Gleaner*, founded in 1863 by Mr. Robert Sellar, author of Gleaner Tales and the History of the County of Huntingdon, etc. The Richmond *Guardian*, founded by W. G. Jones, and known at first as the Richmond County *Advocate;* the St. Francis *Telegraph*, started at Sherbrooke in 1851 by W. L. Felton; the Three Rivers *Inquirer*, founded by G. and R. Lanigan; the Yamaska *News;* the Coaticook *Observer;* the Cowansville *Observer;* the Pontiac *Advance;* and the Three Rivers *Echo* may also be mentioned.

The Province of Quebec has been the stage on which a number of religious papers—more or less controversial in their tendencies—have played their parts. Among them may be mentioned the *Canadian*

Baptist magazine, the *Berean* (Church of England), the *Bible Christian*, edited by the Rev. Dr. John Cordner, brother-in-law of Parkman, the historian; the *True Witness*, edited for some years by Mr. J. C. Clerk, of the family of Clerk of Penicuik (baronets), near Edinburgh, and later by Mr. C. A. McDonnell and Dr. Foran; the *Canada Presbyterian;* the *Protestant;* the *Juvenile Presbyterian*, edited by John Greenshields; the *Echo* and *Protestant Episcopal Recorder*, edited by the Rev. F. B. Tate, and published by Thomas Sellar; the *Church Observer*, edited by a committee of clergymen and published by W. R. Salter; *The Voice of Jacob*, edited by the Rev. A. DeSola, professor of Hebrew and Spanish literature in McGill University, are only a few out of many papers of this class.

In papers devoted to wit, satire, humour, and the comedies of common life, this province has been fairly rich. Among those that sprang to life, blossomed, and decayed when the circumstances that favoured their birth had undergone a change, may be mentioned *Nonsense,* The *Jester,* The *Wasp, Grinchuckle* (a comic *nom de guerre* of the late William Workman, formerly Mayor of Montreal), *Diogenes, Stadacona, Punch, The Gridiron, The Sprite, The Free Lance, The Bee, The Dagger, Paul Pry,* and *Punch in Canada.* This last acquired celebrity during the excitement attending the discussion over the Rebellion Losses Bill and the burning of the Parliament House in Montreal. Lord Elgin received a good deal of satirical attention in it. *The Free Lance* was started by G. T. Lanigan, who was also associated with the beginnings of the Montreal

M. A. JAMES
A Prominent Member of Association
for many years

H. P. MOORE
President 1892

A. F. PIRIE
President 1893

T. H. PRESTON
President 1894

Star. He was subsequently connected with the New York *World* and ended his days in Philadelphia. *Diogenes* was of a higher literary rank than most of the ephemeral sheets of this kind that shot across the literary, social, or political horizon. It was edited by Mr. George Murray, B.A. (Oxon.), an accomplished scholar and well-known poet. The *Spectator*, started by T. D. King, though it lasted only a few weeks, contained some well-written articles on prominent Montrealers of forty years ago, including a portrayal of Lieut.-Col. Chamberlin, C.M.G.

Of legal, medical, commercial, educational, industrial, financial, and special trade journals, the number started from time to time may, in the aggregate, be called legion. Free Masons, Odd Fellows, and Templars of Temperance had also their organs. Of literary magazines the most successful were the *New Dominion Monthly* (John Dougall & Son), the *Canadian Illustrated News* (G. E. Desbarats), the *Saturday Reader* (R. Worthington), the *Hearthstone*, the *Dominion Illustrated Monthly*, the *Student's Monthly* and other college journals; *Canadiana*, a monthly magazine established by Mr. W. J. White, advocate, as the organ of the Society for Historical Studies; the *University Monthly*, representing Toronto, McGill, and Dalhousie Universities; *World Wide*, an eclectic (John Dougall & Son), and the *Standard*, an illustrated weekly, published by the George Murray Company, and of which Mr. F. Yorston is managing editor. Of scientific periodicals there have been a good many from time to time, but the most permanent and valuable is the organ of the Natural History Society of Montreal, now known as the

Record of Science. Mention ought not to be omitted of the publications of the Literary and Historical Society of Quebec, and of the Numismatic and Antiquarian Society of Montreal.

Among the journalists of the Province of Quebec during the first century after the Conquest, there were, as may be gathered from this hasty retrospect, some men of rare endowments and interesting careers. The names of Dr. Waller, John Fleming, Dr. John Charlton Fisher, Thomas Storrow Brown, Charles Roger, the Hon. John Neilson, Mungo Kay, Dr. O'Callaghan, (the Hon. Sir) Francis Hincks, Robert Weir, David Chisholme, L. H. McCullough, S. H. Wilcocke, the Careys, the Middletons, suggest, some of them, taste and learning, others, strong convictions and a determination of purpose that recoiled from no perils. The men who bore those names represented each great division of the Mother Country and they differed widely in their political views. Some of them have left apologies for the decisions at which they arrived at great turning points in their own lives and in the destiny of Canada. We judge them more leniently than they judged each other and try to understand and excuse where we cannot approve. One of them who died at sea and whose body was committed to the deep has left himself a monument in the epitaph he wrote for the foes who received their death wounds on the Plains of Abraham. While Wolfe and Montcalm live in men's memories the name of Dr. John Charlton Fisher cannot be forgotten.

And who were the successors of those pioneers at the time when this narrative opens? We can at least

recall the names of some of them. In the year 1858
Arthur Harvey, Brown Chamberlain, D.C.L., David
Kinnear, Robert Abraham, John Henry Willan, John
Dougall, A. N. Rennie, James Moir Ferris, William
Bristow, Matthew Ryan, Rollo Campbell, Thomas
Carey, J. F. McDonnell, Thomas Darcy McGee,
Edward Goff Penny, E. H. Parsons, John Lowe, were
well-known figures in Lower Canadian journalism.
McGee had just begun that Canadian career which was
to be so fruitful, although it was so sadly cut short.
He began it as a journalist, and we may almost regard
his *New Era* as prophetic, for few laboured more
zealously than he in the cause of Confederation. He
lived to see the new era inaugurated, but not to see the
Dominion completed. Parsons became the fiercest
of champions for the Southern cause. John Dougall was
the advocate of the Northern ideal. They were both
vigorous writers, but Parsons held the most formidable
pen of his day. Practically he was (apart from his
dream of a powerful Southern Confederacy) a free
lance, and was dreaded at times by friend as well as
foe. He was at this time editing the Montreal
Advertiser: later he had charge of the *Evening Telegraph*.

One by one the men who had the lead in the journalism of Quebec when our Association's annals began, disappeared from the places that knew them. Some died
in harness; others entered the civil service and in due
time were pensioned off; others became more or less
prominent figures in the political life of their time. In
their stead others came to the front, of whom some had
learned from them the secrets of their mystery (métier),

and had tried to follow in their footsteps: while others were newcomers who had already made a reputation. It would not be easy to give a list of the more eminent newspaper men of any period or any locality that would be satisfactory to every reader. When the story of Lower Canadian journalism comes, however, to be written by the future historian, certain names are pretty sure to be mentioned, some of which are comprised in the following list :—Hon. Thomas White, John Livingstone, F. E. Molyneux St. John, S. L. Kydd, Frank Carrel, John R. Dougall, E. R. Smith, G. E. Desbarats, Richard White, G. T. Lanigan, Frederick Yorston, Henry Dalby, Hugh Graham, C. H. Parmelee, Russ Huntington, Charles Denroche Barr, George Spaight, C. B. Allardyce, Watson Griffin, G. Krauss, Leslie Thom, A. G. Doughty, John Boyd, John Norris, J. Ferguson, Captain Kirwan, Martin J. Griffin, James Kirby, LL.D., advocate, R. S. White, George Murray, T. Robertson, Smeaton White, T. Marshall, Joseph Walsh, J. S. Brierly, G. Tolley, George Young, John Phillips, John T. Lesperance, J. Corey, J. P. Edwards, G. H. Larminie, Hon. Peter Mitchell, James Stewart, John Wilson, Carroll Ryan, E. J. Duggan, J. C. Cunliffe, Austin Mosher, J. J. Proctor, E. F. Slack, James Harper, Senator Cloran, Charles Marcil, M.P., E. G. O'Connor, George Barnum, J. R. V. Forest, J. Clifford Smith, A. H. U. Colquhoun, D. Browne, T. Bark, H. Mason, Newton MacTavish, M. S. Foley, L. S. Channell, P. D. Ross, J. E. Atkinson, Lyon Cohen, Mrs. Atkinson (" Madge Merton"), Mrs. Everard Cotes (Miss Sara J. Duncan), Mrs. J. Clark Murray, Miss Frazer (author of «Atma"), Miss Charlton, Miss Blanche L. Macdonell, etc. The life story of some of the bearers of the foregoing names could be made not only interesting but instructive and exemplary. They represent various, but by no means all, the activities of successful journalism. Only a few of them learned the newspaper business in its entirety. Some of them planned what others executed. It would not be fair to call any of them mere dilettanti, though to some of them the newspaper was merely a path to what they deemed a more toil-worthy goal. They did not all wield the pen of the ready writer, but most of them had the instinct for discernment and selection which made them good leaders, good lieutenants, or clubbable and efficient co-workers.

In estimating the progress of this section of the Canadian press during half a century, it might first of all be essential to establish what is meant by progress. There are probably as many kinds of progress as there are of glory, even if we leave the stars out of the reckoning. The progress that we have in mind would be that which would result from striking an average. In the material appliances for composition, press-work, the expeditious printing off of big editions of voluminous papers, the change since 1858, when our Association began its career, has been so profound and far-reaching that we hardly know which of the two would furnish the greater surprise—the marvellous contrivances of to-day to the elderly foreman of fifty years ago, or a selection from the presses that then prevailed to the up-to-date superintendent of to-day. Improvements in printing presses which mark a regular evolution, the chief agents of which might be counted on the fingers, have induced corresponding changes in the training of the men and women who work them. The compositor of fifty years ago has become obsolete. The editorial and business staffs of even leading papers in 1858 would be futile for the diversity of departments of their actual successors. We have already referred to the effect of the ocean cable on the destiny of the press. To us of 1908 the paper of 1858 would hardly seem to be a newspaper at all. Yet in some respects the development of our papers in certain directions may be of doubtful value. Of course, much must depend on the point of view. Elderly clergymen or lay moral reformers may sometimes stand aghast when they see papers nominally religious in tone and whose principal aim used to be all kinds of reform largely addicted to horse-shows, foot-ball matches, and the social divagations, and barely stopping short at the prize ring! Then, again, a great deal more space is given to the description of spectacular crime than was once customary, indeed, possible. But, if there are excesses to-day where fifty years ago there were short-comings, there is also unquestioned advance in several ways—in the fairness and fullness of parliamentary and other political reports; in often excellent digests of the business situation from day to day; and in admirable culled or original reading for young and old. Whether the moralist has, on the whole, more reason to be dissatisfied or to be pleased with the position that the British press now occupies in this Province of Quebec, one perhaps may be excused from affirming positively. For our own part, however, we are disposed to take the more hopeful view, and to conclude that the remarkable material progress of the last fifty years has been identified with an intellectual and moral advance that is not out of keeping with it.

JOHN READE.

THE PRESS OF ONTARIO

OF the public press of Ontario, it has been said that
it gives the public far more than it receives, and
that it is capable of serving a community many times
the size of that in which it disseminates the news. That
this opinion is not unfounded, comparisons with the
journalism of Great Britain and the United States
abundantly prove. In both these lands, business centres
of the same strength as to population and wealth as
those of Ontario can boast no such productions as our
city dailies, whether they be "mornings" or "evenings." There, also, the press of the "provinces," to
borrow the English term, is inferior to that portion of
Canada of which we are now speaking. Ontario, as a
matter of fact, has, for the spreading of information
among the people, machinery which, if we take into
consideration the market possibilities for its products,
surpasses that of most English speaking countries.
This situation is to be attributed to the popular relish
for public discussion, which is one of the results of our
system of education, and to the zeal of those who have
made the moulding of public opinion their life work.

It was from small beginnings, and in the face of
difficulties and disappointments, that the excellence of
to-day was attained. The first editor to publish a
paper in what is now Ontario, and what was then
Upper Canada, was a Frenchman, Lewis Roy by

name. This father of Ontario journalism issued his "Salutatory" on the 13th day of April, 1793. How came he to launch upon the troubled sea of newspaperdom at that early date? It appears that the separation of Upper from Lower Canada, and the appointment of Governor Simcoe in 1791 to rule over the new division of the country, gave currency to the view that a great population would soon occupy the new west, and that Newark, the capital, would speedily become an important centre of trade and of industry. Mr. Roy heard of the prospects, and consequently hastened to the promising field to establish his journal under the name of the *Upper Canada Gazette and American Oracle*. High were the aspirations of the publisher. The *Upper Canada Gazette and American Oracle* was to become "the vehicle of intelligence in this growing province of whatever may tend to its interest, benefit, and common advantage." High, also, were the rates for the pioneer journal. The subscription price was three dollars per annum, and the charge for advertising four shillings for twelve lines. Roy's weekly was well printed on good paper. But the enterprising Frenchman could not command a large subscription list among the early settlers; nor was his advertising patronage sufficient to cover his expenses. After a year's trial, therefore, he abandoned the field and made Montreal the scene of his labours. Here he took charge of the Montreal *Gazette*, the paper which Benjamin Franklin had established in the mistaken belief that he could make it a medium for the preaching of antagonism to British institutions. The successor to Lewis Roy was Gideon Tiffany, a printer who united

11

with his journalistic work the business of printing for
the Government. Mr. Tiffany continued the publication until 1799, when, the seat of Government having
been transferred to York, now Toronto, the *Gazette*
followed it to the northern shore of the lake. Tiffany
and his brother, however, remained at Niagara, for
they had confidence in that town, and jointly issued
a successor to the *Gazette*, which they designated the
Canada Constellation, the first number of which was
issued on July 20, 1799. The Messrs. Tiffany intend-
ed to serve the public independently and well. Their
introductory appeal to the people dwelt upon the usefulness and the influence of the press, and deprecated
the "political printer"—referring no doubt to the publishers of the *Gazette*, which had crossed the water with
the Governor, and had become under Messrs. Waters
and Simons, the new proprietors, a species of Government organ. As independent publishers they contended that they could contribute to the unity and the prosperity of the community. Their policy was one of
local loyalty, and they proposed to devote themselves
to the interests of Niagara, rather than to those of York,
the rival town across the lake, whose pretensions they
ridiculed.

Unfortunately, the *Constellation* perished at the end
of the year. Its successor, the *Herald*, holding an
inquest upon the remains, attributed the sudden death
to starvation. The publishers had forgotten to insist
upon payment in advance, and had suffered in consequence. Curiously enough the *Herald*, with the
experience of the *Constellation* before it, fell into the
error which it had detected in its predecessor, and was

able to hold out for but two years. A third enterprise, and still another, followed the *Herald* and the *Constellation*, all dying for want of support. Yet there was some advertising for the active business manager to capture. Here is a sample from the *Niagara Herald* of January 2, 1802:

"For Sale—A negro man slave, 18 years of age, stout and healthy, has had the smallpox, and is capable of work either in the house or outdoors.

"The terms will be made easy to the purchaser, and cash or new lands received in payment. Enquire of the printer."

Of such announcements, however, the Niagara journal did not have the monopoly, for there appear in the York papers of the same period advertisements such as this:

"To be sold.—A healthy, strong negro woman, about thirty years of age, understands cooking and laundry.

"N.B.—She can dress ladies' hair. Enquire of the printer. York, Dec. 20th, 1800."

And again, warnings of the following nature:

"All persons are forbidden from harbouring my slave 'Sal' and will be prosecuted if they keep her half an hour. Charles Field."

It ought to be explained with reference to these notices that while the few slaves brought to the province in early days could be legally held, no additions to the holdings of that nature were permitted. The Legislature at its first session at Niagara proclaimed the introduction of slaves illegal, and slavery died an early and natural death. Niagara turned out to be a graveyard for the infant newspaper. Nor need this be a matter for surprise. With the removal of the seat of Government to York, much of the business of the first capital of Upper Canada slipped away from it. It was to York that the public officials came. It was at York that the Legislature sat. It was in York that the little trade of the new province centred. All that was left to Niagara was the military post and such business as the surrounding country, which was practically unoccupied, afforded. Under the circumstances, the newspaper publisher could not look for a livelihood, much less for comfort, in Governor Simcoe's deserted village. More hopeful was the outlook on the other shore of the lake, where the *Upper Canada Gazette*, first under the management of Messrs. Waters and Simons, and, afterwards, under that of Mr. J. Bennett, was now issued. This paper, however, had its difficulties. One of these was an occasional paper famine which necessitated its publication, sometimes, on wrapping paper, and at other times on the blue paper used for the covers of official reports. Another was the inability to procure the news with which to make the issue attractive and interesting. The *Gazette* depended upon the New York papers, which were very irregular in their arrival, for its British and foreign intelligence, and it passed over local affairs altogether. The whipping or branding of a criminal, according to the custom of those days, would be mentioned, but the public meetings, although duly announced, received no attention, and there was no discussion of public movements.

Until 1818, the *Gazette* was issued. In that year it

came to a sudden stop. The invaders from the United States scattered its type, and destroyed its press. In 1817, however, it was revived by Dr. Horne, an army surgeon, and was subsequently transferred by him to Mr. Charles Fothergill, who changed the name to the *Weekly Register*, under which designation it fought William Lyon Mackenzie and his propaganda. Meanwhile, political discussion called a variety of papers into existence. One that became celebrated was the *Upper Canadian Guardian and Freeman's Journal*, which was launched in 1807 by Joseph Wilcox, a member of the Legislature, and the first leader of the Opposition. Wilcocks was so fiery in his attack, and so relentless in his pursuit of the powers that be, as to achieve martyrdom in the form of imprisonment for breach of privilege. Whatever sympathy may have been extended to him by reason of his incarceration was not of long duration, for in 1812 he deserted to the Americans, and was killed at the siege of Fort Erie, thus proving himself a traitor and an enemy of the continued independence of the Canadian people. Another Opposition journal to become famous was the *Colonial Advocate*, which appeared in May, 1824. Printed at Lewiston, N.Y., dated from Queenston, and circulated in York, the *Colonial Advocate*, under the editorship of William Lyon Mackenzie, was a thorn in the side of the Administration. Removed to York, it became even more objectionable to the ruling men and to the Tory element. At one time the feeling with reference to it was so bitter that its office was raided, and its type thrown into the lake. But it laboured on, with responsible government as the reform for which it struggled. William Lyon Mackenzie was a tremendous worker, and a keen writer; but somewhat impetuous. The resort to arms in 1837 brought the *Colonial Advocate* to its last issue. While Mackenzie's journal was fighting the Government, that authority was not idle in so far as the formation of public opinion was concerned. It had the support of the *Upper Canada Gazette* under Dr. Horne until 1820, when John Carey, the first Canadian Parliamentary reporter, who had reported the debates for the *Gazette*, began the publication of the *Observer* as an organ favourable to the Administration. It also had the assistance of the *Loyalist*, a paper established for the defence of the Government in 1826, and the *Courier*, established by George Gurnett in 1828

The troubles of 1837 seem to be the dividing line between primitive Ontario journalism and the journalism of the mid-century period, for after that date there appeared the moderate Liberal newspaper which called for reforms without advising extreme measures, and the moderate Tory paper which stood by the powers as they existed, but did not antagonize timely changes. Of the former class of journal the *Examiner*, established by Mr. (afterwards Sir Francis) Hincks in 1838, and edited for years by Charles Lindsey, was an early example. Mr. Hincks was a Reformer of the old school, and an earnest advocate of responsible government in the sense in which it was understood by Robert Baldwin. In the same category was the *Banner*, founded in 1843 by Peter Brown, the father of the two distinguished journalists George and J. Gordon Brown, who gave the *Globe*, which was first issued in 1844, and

into which the *Banner* and the *Examiner* were merged,
its character and its name. Of a similar type was
the *North American*, edited by the public man afterwards known to fame as Hon. William Macdougall.
This paper, which first saw the light in 1850, had a
mission and a distinct programme. The union of
Upper and Lower Canada had been accomplished and
responsible government had been conceded. Mr. Macdougall saw there was more to be done, and through
the *North American* he laid down his propositions.
These were fifteen in number. They included a demand for an elective Upper House, for the abolition of
the property qualification for Parliament, for the extension of the franchise to householders, for the ballot
in elections, for representation by population, for the
right of Canada to regulate her commercial intercourse
with other nations, for a decimal currency, and for the
free navigation of the St. Lawrence. It is interesting to
observe that all these reforms were tried, and that some
of them remain with us to this day. Mr. Macdougall's
paper became the mouthpiece of the Administration
formed by Mr. Hincks, the founder of the *Examiner*,
but in 1857, as a result of a new turn in the political
wheel, was amalgamated with the *Globe*, Mr. Macdougall himself joining the staff of that paper as an
editorial writer. Up to this point all the journals
of Liberal proclivities published since the rebellion
centred in the *Globe*, of which Hon. George Brown
was the master mind. The *Globe* flourished under Mr.
Brown up to the time of his assassination by an em-
ploye, and continued its successful career under Mr.
Gordon Brown, Mr. John Cameron, Mr. E. W. Thom-

son, Mr. J. S. Willison, who resigned to take charge of the *News*, and Rev. James A. Macdonald.

On the other side of politics important papers came into existence. In 1838 the *British Colonist* was established by Hugh Scobie, and the *Palladium* by Charles Fothergill, while in 1840 the *Patriot* was introduced by Thomas Dalton. On the death of Mr. Dalton, the *Patriot* was conducted by his widow until 1848, when Col. O'Brien, of Shanty Bay, afterwards a member of Parliament, purchased it. Mr. Lucius O'Brien became the editor and Mr. Samuel Thompson the business manager. One year later Mr. O'Brien sold to Mr. Ogle R. Gowan, a prominent member of the Orange Order, who, with Mr. Thompson, conducted the paper until 1853. In that year the weekly was taken over by Mr. Gowan and the daily became the property of Mr. Thompson. Meanwhile the *Colonist*, under Hugh Scobie, had forged ahead, but it had lost its founder, and was being conducted by his widow. The situation was such as to facilitate the union of the *Daily Patriot* with the *Colonist*, and this amalgamation was accomplished in 1853, when Mr. Thompson, who had become the proprietor of the *Patriot*, bought the *Colonist* and combined the two properties. It is said of the *Colonist* of that period that it was in get-up an exact counterpart of the London *Times*. The size of the sheet, the type, the manner of setting the ads., were all copied from the Thunderer. That it was ably written, there can be no doubt. One of its editors was John Sheridan Hogan, a public man of great power, whose essay on Canada written for the Universal Exhibition of 1856 won the highest commendation.

L. W. SHANNON
President 1895

J. S. BRIERLEY
President 1896

COL. J. B. MACLEAN
President 1897

ROBERT HOLMES
President 1898

Mr. Hogan met with a tragic end. In the winter of 1858 he was missed. It was reported that he had left for Texas. But in the spring his body was found in the Don, where it had been thrown by the Brooks' Bush Gang, a notorious collection of thugs, by whom he had been murdered. Another editor of note was Robert A. Harrison, who afterwards became Chief Justice of Ontario. In 1857 there came a great financial crash, in which Mr. Thompson, the proprietor of the *Colonist*, suffered heavy loss. This necessitated the sale of the paper a year later to Messrs. Sheppard & Morrison. These proprietors afterwards sold to the publisher of the *Leader*, Mr. James Beaty. The *Leader* had been established in 1852 as a Conservative journal, and was vigorously managed under Mr. Charles Lindsey, its editor. After taking over the *Colonist*, it became a strong force. It, however, met with competition, its earliest opponent being the *Telegraph*, which was started in 1866 by Mr. John Ross Robertson, now the proprietor of the *Telegram*. This paper flourished until 1876. Meanwhile a new Conservative daily had come into existence—the *Mail*— in 1872. The *Mail* was founded through the exertions of Mr. Thomas C. Patteson, a friend and admirer of the two Macdonalds, John A. and John Sandfield. He was aided by Charles Belford and George Gregg, the former editor, and the latter Parliamentary reporter, of the *Leader*. The purpose of the *Mail* was to give strength to the Conservative party, and to advocate the principle of protection which was popularly described as the National Policy. Along these lines it worked, the chief writers being Mr. Patteson, Mr.

Belford, Mr. William Rattray, Mr. Edward Farrer, and Mr. John Maclean, father of Mr. W. F. Maclean, M.P. In 1877 the *Mail* became the property of Mr. John Riordon, of St. Catharines, and Christopher W. Bunting was appointed as its manager. Edward Farrer and Martin J. Griffin were successively its editors. On the death of Mr. Bunting the management passed to Mr. W. J. Douglas, with Arthur Wallis as editor. In the meantime, however, an evolution had taken place in respect of this paper. In 1885 it came into controversy with Sir John Macdonald on the Riel issue, and the allied question of the position of the French race in Canada. This breach widened, and Sir John in 1887 established as the mouthpiece of the Conservative party the *Empire*, under the direction of Mr. David Creighton, with Mr. John Livingstone as its first editor-in-chief, and Mr. A. H. U. Colquhoun as his successor. The *Empire* was vigorously conducted, and was a growing force in the land. In 1895 it was amalgamated with the *Mail*, and the two journals were thereafter known as the *Mail and Empire*. Long before the establishment of the *Empire* there was another candidate for public favour—the *Toronto World*. This daily was founded during a bye-election in West Toronto in the year 1879, with Messrs. W. F. Maclean, Archibald Blue, and Albert Horton as its proprietors. From small beginnings it assumed large proportions, and through the withdrawal of the other partners, became the exclusive property of Mr. Maclean.

The era of the present-day evening paper began in 1873 with the *Sun*, a short-lived venture. This journal was succeeded in 1876 by the *Telegram*. Mr. John

Ross Robertson, its founder, saw that with the growing city population there was a field for a city paper as distinguished from a provincial paper. He therefore made the *Telegram* strongly local, applying it in an especial sense to the discussion of municipal concerns. To the initial success of this journal Mr. A. F. Pirie, its first editor, powerfully contributed. Mr. John Robinson, his successor, has by his ability and versatility added to the popularity of the enterprise. The second of the evenings to enter the field was the *Evening News*, which was established as the afternoon edition of the *Mail* in 1880. This paper was ultimately divorced from the *Mail*. Under the editorship of Mr. E. E. Sheppard it was an aggressive radical publication advocating many changes. It was subsequently managed by Mr. William Douglas, and edited by Mr. H. C. Hocken. In 1904 Mr. J. S. Willison, who had edited the *Globe* with distinction, took charge of the *News*, and conducted it as a journal of the more advanced type for the independent discussion of political, educational, and social matters. The *Evening Star* came into existence in 1893, and ultimately passed under the management of Mr. J. E. Atkinson, when it achieved success. The *Star* had for some years Mr. Joseph T. Clark as chief editorial writer, and on the withdrawal of Mr. Clark, who became the editor of *Saturday Night*, he was succeeded by Mr. John Lewis.

While the press of the capital city was growing that of "the provinces" or of the cities and towns of Upper Canada was making rapid headway. The eastern end of the province, owing to the fact that it was the first section to be occupied, led in journalistic

enterprise. As early as 1801 there appeared in Kingston the *Gazette* under the management of Messrs.
Miles & Kendall, formerly of Montreal. This paper
continued to publish until the war of 1812—a period
during which there ought to have been no end of copy
—when its suspension was regarded as necessary. It
resumed after the war under the name of the *Gazette
and Religious Advocate*, and is supposed to have been
the first religious weekly in America. It ante-dates
the *Christian Guardian*, established in Toronto by Rev.
Dr. Ryerson in 1829. Kingston is the home of long-
lived journalism. There in 1810 the *Chronicle*, afterwards the *News*, and now the *Standard*, was established.
In 1851 the *News* became a daily, and it has served the
public in that capacity ever since. The *Whig* was
launched in 1834 by Dr. F. J. Barker. It passed to
Mr. M. L. Pense, and is now the property of Mr. E.
J. B. Pense, M.P.P., the grandson of the founder.
This journal is one of the few that have remained in
the family by which they were founded. While the
Kingston *News*, now the *Standard*, is the oldest of the
Eastern Ontario papers, the Brockville *Recorder* is the
next in the order of seniority. This journal was established in 1820 by Col. D. Wylie, known to his com-
rades in later years as the father of the Ontario press,
and is the property of Hon. George P. Graham, the
Minister of Railways and Canals. The first paper to
be printed in the district lying between Kingston and
York was the Hallowell *Free Press*, which appeared on
Dec. 28th, 1830. Hallowell was the Picton of to-day.
The chief town of Prince Edward County, it must
have been a busy place at the time when lake naviga-

tion was the principal means of communication between the East and the West. In the opening number of this paper, we get some idea of the conditions under which newspapers were begun in those early days. The editor says: "A number of attempts have been made to publish a journal in this country, proposals circulated, subscriptions obtained to a considerable amount, and the expectations of the public wrought up to the highest degree. Yet every attempt has proved abortive except the present. Repeated imposition has, no doubt, had a tendency to create in the public mind a spirit of indifference and apathy respecting newspapers." Evidently the business of the genuine newspaper man was handicapped by the work of speculators who collected subscriptions on the promise that they would start local journals, but failed to go any farther. Joseph Wilson, who founded the Hallowell *Free Press*, began to print from a wooden press of his own design and secured an iron press from the United States one year later. In 1840 the Prince Edward *Gazette* began to be published. This paper became the Picton *Gazette* in 1847, and has been issued regularly ever since. Its contemporary, the Picton *Times* came into existence a few years later. Belleville was one of the pioneer newspaper towns east of Toronto. Its first paper was the *Anglo-Canadian*, commenced in 1831. Of this journal the *Ontario* is the descendant. In September, 1834, George Benjamin began the publication of the *Intelligencer*. This gentleman was an Englishman of more than ordinary ability, and a strong Conservative. He issued the paper, ran for Parliament, and was a member from 1856 to 1863. On his death a young man who had entered his office as a "devil" succeeded him in the management of the paper, and in the representation of the county. This individual was Mackenzie Bowell, afterwards a Minister of the Crown, a senator, a knight, and Premier of the Dominion.

Western Canada, or the district west of Toronto, had a few little papers in the "thirties," but no publications of permanent or substantial character were issued until the "forties." The first paper to be established early and to last long was the Hamilton *Spectator*. By Robert Reid Smiley the *Spectator* was founded, and its first number came out on July 15, 1846. The paper was Conservative, but independent and progressive. It advocated many reforms, among them the secularization of the Clergy Reserves. On the death of Mr. Smiley in 1855, John Smiley and William Gillespie became the owners. But these gentlemen were hit by the business depression and were compelled to part with the property. The new proprietors were Thomas and Richard White, who took possession in 1864. These experienced newspaper men made the *Spectator* a success; but soon removed to Montreal, where, in a wider field, they published the *Gazette*. In 1873 William Southam and William Carey took control. Under their management, in co-operation with such writers as David McCullough, A. T. Freed, and J. Robson Cameron, the *Spectator* prospered. The Hamilton *Times*, a vigorous Liberal paper, for years edited by H. F. Gardner, was a later candidate for public recognition. It was first issued in 1858. The *Herald*, independent, is still more recent. It was founded in 1889. London's first permanent newspaper was established in 1849. There had been a printing plant at St. Thomas with which Thomas Watson Woodward printed an occasional paper of the Reform type. In 1837 Woodward abandoned journalism and joined the militia. He is said to have declared that while a Reformer he was not a rebel. His plant found its way to London, and was bought by William Sutherland, who in 1849 started the *Free Press*. In 1852 Josiah and Stephen Blackburn bought the paper, running it as a weekly until 1855, when it became a daily. For years Mr. M. G. Bremner has been the editorial manager. The *Advertiser* was founded by John Cameron in 1863. An advanced journal of Liberal views, it speedily won public favour. It has been edited by Mr. Cameron himself, by Hon. David Mills, and by Mr. M. Rossie. Brantford received the benefit of the public press early in its career. The *Courier* was established by Mr. Henry Lemmon in 1834, and the *Expositor*, now the property of Mr. T. H. Preston, M.P.P., in 1852. It is not possible within moderate space to follow the history of journalism in Ontario in all its phases, or to do justice to every publication now being issued, and to every worker in the great publicity field. For this reason this review is confined to the story of the pioneers. These enterprising men commenced their work amidst many drawbacks; but left behind them a public taste for current literature which is the most valuable asset of the journalism of to-day.

ARTHUR WALLIS.

REMINISCENCES OF 1856.

I FIRST knew Toronto in 1856. The dailies were the *Globe, Colonist,* and *Leader.* It is a mistake to suppose the *Globe* owed its pre-eminence to its politics. It was due to its excellence as a purveyor of news. It recorded everything of public interest and did so promptly. There was a trial of a physician at Cobourg for murder. A reporter was sent who telegraphed his notes, which meant heavy cost. In collecting news the *Globe* far outdistanced the two other papers, and even people who did not like its politics read it first.

Its excellence in this regard was due to Gordon Brown, who really made the reputation of the *Globe,* for while his brother's personality stamped it in public repute, it was Gordon's work that put it in the front rank. He was a silent, observant man, who led, so it impressed me, a lonesome life. His capacity for work was great, and he was unwearied in making each number of the *Globe* the best possible with the means at hand.

His first assistant I knew was James K. Edwards, probably the best stenographer Canada has known. He died in Washington, where he was head of the Congressional staff. Edwards had a rare faculty of paragraphing and condensing, and nothing in the papers escaped him His watchfulness of the news columns of the *Globe* was unceasing. He always accompanied George Brown on his political tours and reported his speeches verbatim. They were never published, however, as he wrote them. Brown carefully went over them, changing and adding in a way that, boy-like, I did not think was morally right, for I thought they should have been printed as they were spoken. Even trivial utterances, on occasions of no importance, had to be thus submitted to him and revised. Brown did little work on the paper, indeed was seldom in the editorial room. He was much away at Bothwell, where he had land and mills, and in attending political gatherings. When at home he always had a succession of visits from people of all sorts, for he kept in touch with each constituency of the province, and had really no time for the paper, to the business branch of which he paid more attention than to the literary. His articles can always be picked out by their big type and prodigality of italic, exclamation points, and capitals. From what I know, I should say Gordon was the maker of the *Globe*. Though George left the editing of the paper to his brother he impressed upon it features Gordon did not care for. Theatrical performances were neither reported nor advertised, nor were horse races and the like. Work was suspended on Saturday at midnight, a few compositors, by rotation, returning at midnight Monday morning.

The *Globe's* chief competitor was the *Colonist*, which, in 1856 and later on, had a strong hold on the public, which it lost from being poorly managed and its strong dependence on Government support. The *Leader* never was a paper of the people, and had little support outside Conservative circles. It introduced, if I am not mistaken, in 1860, the cent daily.

It was a small sheet printed on straw paper. Instantly there sprang up another novelty to Toronto—the newsboy—and every afternoon, about 4 o'clock, the streets resounded with, "Here ye are for the *Ev-ning Lee-dar!*" I have a pleasant recollection of it from reading in its columns, where it was reproduced as a serial, "Tom Brown at Oxford."

Of the other papers little need be said. The *Mirror* was a Catholic paper, poorly printed and got up. The *Message* was a curiosity, dotted with cuts of roosters and all sorts of old pictures that had accumulated in its office. It made no pretension to give the news, and what was original was personal items about the editor. Mackenzie was ill-balanced, and his morbid egotism led him to criticize whatever jarred on his notions. To speak of him as a newspaper man is absurd. The *Message* had no regular publishing day and appeared when it was ready.

Another fake paper was the *Times*, published by a Mr. Hope, who was a well-known character. He was a little man, with a squeaky voice, who haunted the post-office, and was known by the sub-title of his paper, the *Old Countryman*. He was English, and everything that was not English was wrong. He boarded at the Queen's and toadied after the politicians, getting much profitable advertising for his paper, which had no circulation outside the city.

I cannot give the date when the *Grumbler* appeared —'59 or '60 I should say. It was the first successful *literary* paper Canada had and the best. I say literary, for in its first three volumes will be found much clever writing. As its founders dropped off it fell into inferior hands, and its humor became mechanical. The Conservatives started opposition to it, the *Poker*. It was well named, for it had no more wit or humor in it than a poker.

Of the country press it is to be noted that it had no existence worth mentioning until 1851, and if you examine the title pages of papers now published few will be found that existed before that year. The reason of this was the rates of postage. On their being modified a swarm of country papers started. It was not difficult ; a few hundred dollars was sufficient. I knew of papers whose plants did not cost $300. They were as a rule poor affairs, yet better than their support warranted. Places that are towns and cities now were villages then, and it was easier to obtain subscribers than to collect subscriptions. Conservative papers were liberally dealt with in getting official advertisements, the Government check often paying the paper maker. Many worthy printers wore out their lives in the struggle to establish papers in places that could not give adequate support. In some points the country papers of that time were superior to those of the present. Nearly all their proprietors having come from the Old Land, their ideal of a newspaper was the British press: those of to-day are imitators of the American. There was none of the wretched gossip that passes now for local news, and their columns were not sewers into which every passer-by could pitch items.

In this one regard, that they did not minister to the vanity of their readers nor intrude into the privacy of the home, I hold these old-time journalists in respect.

They tried to have an editorial in each number and reported whatever was of public interest without exaggeration, and in better English than their successors. The best printed and the best prepared of the country papers was the Sarnia *Observer*, and after it the Barrie *Advance*. The worst printed and edited was Kirby's paper, the Niagara *Mail*. The poverty of these publishers of country papers half a century ago made them the servants of their party and of the big man of their constituencies. There were exceptions, where men earnestly strove to mould public opinion on the lines they believed were true. The editorial style of the time I speak of was quite pretentious, and writers whose knowledge of Latin did not go beyond the delectus were fond of learned quotations, preferable to the flippancy and would-be smartness that too many aim at now.

It used to be the rule, that the man who published a paper was a practical printer, and the general belief was that no publisher could be successful who was not. An amusing illustration of this was a fond father entering the *Globe* office one forenoon with his son, and telling Mr. Brown the boy was ambitious of being an editor. "All right," was the reply, "the first step is to give him a general knowledge of printing: send him down to-morrow morning." When the lad appeared he was detailed to roll for a hand-press—two rolls and distribute—damn yer eyes—with added instructions as to the brayer. When six o'clock came he went home to his mother daubed hands and face and shirt with ink. He did not return to his editorial class.

R. Sellar.

HISTORY OF THE MANITOBA PRESS

THE first newspaper in what was known as Rupert's Land, and long prior to the transfer of the North-West Territories to Canada, was called the *Nor-Wester*. It owed its inception to the enterprise of two well-known Ontario newspaper men, who came from Toronto in the autumn of 1859; Wm. Buckingham and Wm. Coldwell. The former came as a representative of the Toronto *Globe*, and the latter as a correspondent of the *Leader*.

The first issue of the *Nor-Wester* is dated the 28th Dec., 1859, and was published at Fort Garry, a mere hamlet, yet the Chief Post of the Hudson's Bay Company in this country. They brought their outfit along with them, and had a somewhat rugged experience in its transport from St. Paul to Fort Garry by the transport system then in vogue via Red River cart. A file of this paper is in the reference section of the Provincial Library, and a perusal of it brings up many fond reminiscences of the early history of the country. It was a four-page weekly with quite a lot of advertisements, well selected Canadian and foreign news; its leaders, too, were ably written, and had much to do with the early development of Manitoba and its subsequent transfer to the Dominion of Canada.

Mr. Buckingham's connection with the paper lasted only a year, as he returned East to assume charge of a paper in Stratford. He afterwards became private secretary to the Hon. Alex. Mackenzie during the Liberal regime at Ottawa from 1873 till 1878. Mr. Coldwell continued to edit the newspaper, and took into partnership with him Mr. James Ross, a relative, and son of the late Alex. Ross, author of several volumes on the Western Country. James Ross, although a native of the Red River Settlement, had quite a penchant for literature. He was educated at St. John's College, Red River, and Toronto University, where he graduated with honours in 1857. He was classical master in Upper Canada College in 1858. He returned to Fort Garry in 1859, where he became Postmaster and Sheriff. It was about this time, too, he became identified with the *Nor-Wester*, which he edited and partly owned from 1860 till 1864. Mr. Ross severed his connection with the paper at this date to become associate editor of the Hamilton *Spectator*, and was also a writer in the Toronto *Globe*. He was admitted to the Bar of Manitoba in 1870, and became Chief Justice during the Provisional Government of Louis Riel. He died 20th September, 1871. The *Nor-Wester* after 1864 was published by Messrs. Coldwell and Schultz, but the former retired in 1865, and the paper was afterwards published by Dr. Schultz until 1870. Wm. Coldwell went to Toronto in 1865, but returned again to the Red River in 1870, and was about to embark upon another journalistic venture, the *Red River Pioneer*, but only the outside pages were printed, when Riel pounced upon the plant and confiscated it to his own use.

Upon the wreck of the *Pioneer*, Riel started the *New Nation*, with H. M. Robinson, an American, and a member of his Provisional Government, as editor. This journal had but an ephemeral existence for eight months, and ceased publication with the advent of the troops under Sir Garnet Wolseley in September, 1870. It is perhaps only fair to Riel to say, that shortly after seizing the plant of the *Pioneer*, he compensated Mr. Coldwell for the loss he sustained in connection with his venture to start the *Red River Pioneer*. The veteran Coldwell, who had lived a retired life for some twenty years, died in February, 1907, having left behind him the imprint of yeoman service as a journalist in the great West. The *Manitoban*, another weekly journal, has to be linked with the name of the late Mr. Coldwell, who had R. Cunningham, who came to the West as correspondent of the Toronto *Globe*, associated with him in this new enterprise, which started in 1870. It ran for two years, when it became the victim of disaster. A mob wrecked the office, and at the same time the offices of the *Nor-Wester* and *Le Metis*, a French paper started by the late Hon. Joseph Royal. The *Manitoban* and *Le Metis* were resurrected, the former merged ultimately into the *Free Press*, and the latter ceased publication in 1882.

There are four other names that must be mentioned in connection with early journalism in this country, and those are: Messrs. W. F. Luxton, P. G. Laurie, Stewart Mulvey, and Hon. Frank Oliver. All four were identified with journalism at Winnipeg in the early seventies. Mr. Luxton started the *Free Press* in 1872, Mr. Laurie published the *News Letter* about 1875, an interesting little sheet, but it lasted only about a year. He subsequently took up his residence in Battleford, the first capital of the North-West Territories, and there, in 1878, started the *Saskatchewan Herald*. This paper still survives the demise of Mr. Laurie, who died over a year ago, at his adopted home, in the far off Saskatchewan, much of whose development is due to the virile pen wielded by this veteran journalist.

The name of Major Stewart Mulvey is strongly interwoven with the texture of early development in Manitoba. He came out as an officer with the Ontario Battalion of the Wolseley Expedition of 1870, and after the Rebellion was over, settled in Winnipeg. Being of an active and vigorous temperament, he at once identified himself with the growth and development of Manitoba. He was much associated with the promotion of education, and although not an expert journalist, yet he contributed largely to the press in the discussion of public questions of the day. He also established a journal called the *Liberal*, in 1871, but it only lived about two years, there being evidently sufficient papers already in the field to supply the demand. Mr. Mulvey joined the Civil Service, being for many years collector of Inland Revenue at Winnipeg. He was greatly devoted to military matters, and went out in the Rebellion of 1885, as Major of the 95th Battalion. He was a politician too, having unsuccessfully contested Selkirk for the House of Commons in 1882. He subsequently sat for one term in the local Legislature. In later years he became Secretary-Treasurer of the Board of Public School Trustees. His death took place at Vancouver on the 25th of May,

W. S. DINGMAN
President 1899

A. G. F. MACDONALD
President 1901

D. McGILLICUDDY
President 1902

H. J. PETTYPIECE
President 1903

1908, and he was buried in Winnipeg, where a large public funeral bore testimony to his popularity.

Hon. Frank Oliver worked for a time as a printer on the Winnipeg *Free Press*, and wrote at intervals for both it and Eastern papers. He was born at Brampton, Peel County, Ontario, in 1853, and came to Manitoba in the early seventies. He migrated to the West in 1880, taking up his residence in Edmonton. He became a member of the North-West Council in 1883, and was elected after to the Assembly, in which he sat from 1888 to 1896. He was next elected to the House of Commons, and now enjoys the distinguished honour of being Minister of the Interior in the Laurier Cabinet. It is, however, as a journalist that he must be noted. He started the Edmonton *Bulletin* in December, 1880, the first volume of which is not much larger than a primer, and for a copy of which ten dollars was paid, for the Provincial Library. It has since become one of the leading journals of the Province of Alberta, with an extensive circulation and generous advertising patronage. Hon. Mr. Oliver owes much of his popularity and success in public life to the able and fearless way in which he conducted the editorial columns of this journal.

The Manitoba *Free Press*, established in 1872 as a weekly, with a daily edition in 1878, has been one of the most successful newspapers in Canada as a business venture, and to-day is one of the leading journals of the Dominion. The name of the late William F. Luxton is indelibly connected with the founding of this great enterprise, and much credit is due him for the success which has attended it since its inception. Mr.

Luxton was born in Devonshire, England, in 1844, and came to Canada when eleven years of age, settling in St. Thomas, Ontario, where he subsequently taught school. He started a newspaper in Strathroy called the *Age*. He sold this paper and next founded the *Huron Expositor*, at Seaforth, one of the leading journals in Western Ontario. Mr. Luxton migrated to Manitoba in 1871, having come out as correspondent for the Toronto *Globe*. He taught the first public school in Fort Garry, but for only one year. His penchant for journalism having revived, he conceived the idea of starting a newspaper in the West, and hence the origin of the *Free Press* in 1872 by Kenny & Luxton. The rapid growth of the West and the necessity for the enlargement of this newspaper prompted Mr. Luxton to make it a joint-stock concern, and attached to it was a large job printing establishment. This marked an epoch which ensured the future success of the enterprise. All, however, did not go well with the original promoter. The control of the stock fell into the hands of political and commercial syndicates who desired a certain policy from the paper. This, Mr. Luxton, as managing editor, could not see his way clear to pursue, as he deemed the policy desired adverse to the interests of the people. His independent attitude cost him dearly, for he lost his interest in the concern, and retired from the paper altogether, very much chagrined at the loss of an enterprise which was his own creation. The newspaper has since been re-organized under new auspices, the owners having erected one of the finest printing houses in Canada. It is the organ of the Liberal party in Western Canada, and wields a large influence in Manitoba and the adjoining Provinces. Mr. Luxton has held many public offices both municipal and Parliamentary, and was largely identified with the progress and rapid development of his adopted Province. He was managing editor of the St. Paul *Globe* for several years, but ill-health compelled him to retire from the position. He returned to Winnipeg in 1901, taking a position in the Civil Service of the Province, which he retained until the time of his death in May, 1907. He was accorded a public funeral and his death was greatly lamented by the entire community.

It might be as well just here to enumerate some other newspaper ventures that for a time shed a dim lustre in the community, but soon after found a journalistic graveyard, owing to a plethora of newspapers, in advance of the demands of the population. Capt. G. F. Carruthers started the *Manitoba Gazette* in 1872, but it lasted only a year. Alex. Begg started the *Trade Review* the same year, but its career came to an end in less than twelve months. Mr. E. L. Barber revived the old *Nor-Wester*, but it lived only a couple of years. Molyneux St. John started the *Weekly Standard* in 1874, but in about a year it was merged in the *Free Press*. W. G. Fonseca started the *Manitoba Weekly Herald* in 1877, but its career was of short duration. Henry J. Clarke started another *Gazette* in 1879, but it survived only a few months. A comic weekly, *Quiz*, started in 1878 by some unknown publisher, created some excitement in the town for over a year, with its somewhat caustic references to the public men of the day. Mr. Nursey started the *Manitoba Telegraph*, but it, too, like its predecessors, was consigned to an early tomb.

The first real live paper, however, to rival the *Free Press*, was one established early in 1879, by C. R. Tuttle. It was called the *Times*, and had both daily and weekly editions. Its advent was concurrent with the return to power of the Sir John A. Macdonald Government, and it espoused the policy of the Conservative party. It started with a fair capital and under favourable auspices, but the expenses of maintenance being in excess of its revenue, and in advance of the requirements of the Province, it got into financial difficulties in about a year. In the interim George H. Ham, now of Montreal, started the *Tribune* ostensibly to supplant the C. R. Tuttle enterprise. The plant of the latter establishment was, however, bought early in 1880 by Amos Rowe, of Ottawa, and the *Times* was revived, in the interest of the Conservative party. Messrs. Rowe and Ham consolidated their interests and the *Tribune* was merged in the *Times*, Mr. Ham taking the editorial management of the joint establishment. This continued up to 1885, when Mr. Rowe retired to become Lands Agent and Customs Officer at Calgary. The *Times* next fell into the hands of a company, and the name was changed to the *Manitoban*. It followed up the policy of its predecessor, and was Conservative in politics. Another change took place in the paper in 1887, when the name was changed to the *Morning Call*, and was under direction of Acton Burrows as managing editor. Upon the retirement of Mr. Burrows in 1890, the paper underwent another change, and with it a new name, the *Nor-Wester*. Geo. H. Ham accepted the position of managing editor. Everything moved along smoothly until 1900, when a new company was formed,

and the name again changed to the *Telegram*, under
the direction of James Hooper, now Deputy Provincial
Secretary and King's Printer of Manitoba, who was
followed shortly after by Sanford Evans as managing
editor.

The independent press has not been without repre-
sentation in this country, for as early as 1882, W. H.
Nagle, an Ottawa journalist, started a paper called the
News, which he subsequently changed to the *Sun*, but
this enterprise did not last over two or three years.
T. H. Preston, now of the *Expositor*, of Brantford,
Ontario, started a new *Sun* which was conducted for a
number of years with some ability and financial success.
Mr. Preston sold out his interest in the *Sun* to the
Manitoban Printing Company, and the paper was
merged into a new journal, already referred to above,
and known as the *Manitoban*. Another journal known
as the *Evening News* was started by W. T. Thompson,
formerly of the *Times* staff, but since connected with
the Duluth *Tribune*. It, however, succumbed to the
inevitable fate of many other papers in less than a year.
R. L. Richardson, who had been upon the editorial
staff of the *Sun*, launched a new enterprise upon the
journalistic stage in 1901, and called it the Winnipeg
Tribune, and it, like its confreres, the *Free Press* and
Telegram, survives to the present day. At the outset
this paper was Liberal, but after the *Free Press* became
the Liberal organ the *Tribune* changed to an independent paper. Many prominent men have been
identified with the press of Manitoba in a journalistic
capacity since the advent of the newspaper to Western
Canada. A few names have been already mentioned

but there are others besides, whose names have only to be mentioned to be remembered favorably in this connection—E. F. F. Brokovski now of Battleford, Saskatchewan; G. B. Elliott, late of Regina; J. R. Cameron, late of Hamilton *Spectator;* E. Farrer, now of Ottawa; A. C. Campbell, R. Houston, of Toronto; J. P. Robertson, Legislative Library, Winnipeg; E. W. Thomson, now of Boston; C. W. Allen, Wm. Dennis, now of Halifax; Fred C. Wade, now of Vancouver; W. E. McLellan, of Halifax, J. Kernighan, "The Khan," of Toronto; G. B. Brooks, of London, England; Lud K. Cameron, now King's Printer, Toronto; D. J. Beaton, formerly of Orillia, Ontario; Arch. McNee, of Windsor, Ontario; R. Moss, late of Toronto; J. C. McLagan, late of Vancouver *World;* Nicholas Flood Davin, late of the Regina *Leader;* Thos. Collins, of Portage la Prairie, now of Summerland, B.C.; Chas. Douglas, of Emerson, now of Vancouver, B.C.; G. F. Galbraith, late of Morden *Monitor;* C. Cliffe, of Portage la Prairie; and W. J. White, formerly of the Brandon *Sun.* There are others whose names do not occur to me just now, but the names of the managing editors of the three large Winnipeg dailies cannot very well be overlooked: J. W. Dafoe, of the *Free Press;* W. E. Nichols, of the *Telegram,* and J. J. Moncrieff, of the *Tribune.*

In conclusion allow me to pay a high compliment to the press of Western Canada, for without it, this country could never have reached the stage of development which it now enjoys. The fourth estate in the West compares favourably with that of the press in any other part of Canada or the United States. When you take into consideration that thirty years ago there was but one newspaper in the small hamlet then known as Fort Garry, and that to-day there are thirty monthly publications, twenty-five semi-weekly papers, two hundred and fifty weekly newspapers, and thirty dailies in Western Canada from Lake Superior to the Pacific Coast, and with a population less than a million souls, you will be able to form some conception of the magnitude of the community and the intelligence of the people to whom the press caters. The first Press Association in the West was formed early in 1882, with the writer as President and Lud. K. Cameron, who founded the *Nor-West Farmer* at Winnipeg that year, as secretary. This Association had the pleasure of a visit from the Canadian Press Association in August, 1882. The Club treated their guests to a sail down the Red River some forty miles, to where it empties into Lake Winnipeg. The mayor and corporation of Winnipeg entertained them afterwards to a drive around the then young city, and to a sumptuous banquet. The Canadian Pacific Railway authorities next treated the visitors to a ride over the Canadian Pacific Railway to Regina, and some six miles further west, where they honoured President Pense in naming a station after him, the mother of Lud. K. Cameron, secretary of the Winnipeg Press Club, performing the baptismal service.

The Western Canada Press Association is still kept up, and has now become a large organization covering a large field. J. W. Dafoe, of the *Free Press*, is honorary president for 1908; C. D. McPherson, of the Portage la Prairie *Graphic*, is president; G. H. Saults, publisher of *Town Topics*, secretary; and John Stovel, of the *Nor-West Farmer*, treasurer. The other officers and executive are all representative of the leading newspapers of the West, and they have succeeded in making the Western Canada Press Association a pretty live institution.

J. P. ROBERTSON,
Provincial Librarian.

IN ALBERTA AND SASKATCHEWAN

SOON after the "great lone land" became part of the Dominion of Canada, and the provisional districts of Assiniboia, Saskatchewan, and Alberta were organized under the general name North-West Territories, Hon. David Laird became our first Lieutenant-Governor, and established temporary quarters at Battleford. The late P. G. Laurie followed closely the trend of events, and was on the spot with his printing press almost simultaneously with the Lieutenant-Governor and his suite. Thus did Mr. Laurie become the pioneer journalist of the vast territories now composing the two prairie provinces of Saskatchewan and Alberta. Mr. Laurie established the Saskatchewan *Herald*, which he personally conducted until his death, only a few years ago.

Frank Oliver, who is now the Hon. Minister of the Interior, was a close second to Mr. Laurie as a pioneer journalist. Mr. Oliver carted his outfit from Winnipeg to Edmonton, a distance of seven hundred miles, across the prairie trails by ox cart. For many years Mr. Oliver personally conducted the smallest and the dearest paper in Canada, the Edmonton *Bulletin*. To-day the *Bulletin* is an eight-page daily, ably conducted and giving the world's news as early and promptly as its closest competitor.

The third newspaper venture was that of C. E. D. Wood, who established the *Gazette* at Fort Macleod in 1882. For fourteen years Mr. Wood remained in charge as editor and proprietor, and although he has since entered the legal profession at Regina, the paper which he founded still flourishes in the old military post, now known as the town of Macleod.

These were the three pioneer journalists who preceded railway extension and braved all the difficulties and other discouragements of their day.

In 1882 the Canadian Pacific Railway reached Regina on the morning of August 23rd. The late Nicholas Flood Davin was one of many visitors to the place soon after. Being a well known litterateur and journalist, and Regina having then been chosen as the seat of Territorial Government, Mr. Davin decided at once to identify himself with the future of the Territories, and announced his decision to establish the Regina *Leader*. Decision soon ripened into action, and the brilliant thoughts of its talented founder soon found expression in the columns of his own paper, which circulated far and wide and increased both his own fame and the fame of Western Canada.

Two other papers established in the early history of the country were, the Qu'Appelle *Vidette*, by the Proctor Bros., and the Moosomin *Courier*, by Beers & Nulty.

The Calgary *Herald* is also a long established journal, and was at one time edited by the late John Livingstone, a veteran journalist who had served some years on different newspapers in Eastern Canada.

In 1885 C. J. Atkinson founded the Regina *Journal*.

In 1891 the *Journal* plant was sold to a company and became the Regina *Standard*, which is now the property of J. K. McInnis & Sons, issuing in semi-weekly and daily editions. The *Standard* is the pioneer daily of the Province of Saskatchewan.

Almost all publishers in the prairie provinces are members of the Western Canada Press Association, and several very pleasurable excursions have been held.

The press has certainly kept pace with the general progress of the West, and there is now a weekly paper in almost every hamlet between the Red River and the Rocky Mountains.

The daily press is also well represented. There are two dailies in Regina, two in Saskatoon, and two in Moose Jaw. Edmonton, the capital of Alberta, has two dailies; Calgary three and Lethbridge one. Western business men are good advertisers, and the general public good subscription patrons. The field, however, is very fully covered at present, but doubtless there will be room for more as population increases and new districts become opened up.

J. K. McINNIS.

IN BRITISH COLUMBIA

FROM the number of newspapers which have come and gone in British Columbia in fifty years, that province may be described as a journalistic cemetery. Throughout the expanse of territory bounded by the Rocky Mountains on the eastern side, the Pacific Ocean on the western side, the Skeena River on the north, and the international boundary line on the south, there are scattered profusely the remains of ambitious pioneer journals. Away back in the early Cariboo days, Messrs. Allan and Lambert (the latter still lives in the town of Chatham, Ontario) "packed" up the long trail that leads from Yale to Williams Creek the plant upon which the Cariboo *Sentinel* was printed. It was a small, four-paged paper, it sold for a dollar a copy, the editor got $150 a week, and no advertisement, however small, was inserted for less than $5.00 per issue. Among its most celebrated contents were "Sauny's Letters Hame." These were in the form of verse and were written by a very clever Scotchman named Anderson, and described, in a graphic and humorous way, the early and true life of the first and greatest mining camp British Columbia ever possessed. The news is principally of the mining camps of Cariboo, but there are occasional belated news of all kinds, and some miscellany. I got the only file that exists from

Lambert when I came to British Columbia years ago, and it is now deposited in the Provincial Library at Victoria. That was one of the few papers in British Columbia which "paid" from the grass roots until the mining industry of Cariboo began to decline and the population dwindle away. It expired of sheer inanition. The plant—I may be mistaken—was removed afterwards to Kamloops to start the Kamloops *Sentinel.* One of the editors, Mr. Geo. Wallace, was a very well-known writer of his day. If we except the coast cities of British Columbia—Victoria, Vancouver, New Westminster and Nanaimo, and it is true to a considerable extent of these in the earlier days—the history of journalism has been the history of pioneering and townsiting. I could give you a list of fifty places offhand that have had newspapers that do not possess them now. I once tried to keep track of them for the purpose of preserving files for the Provincial Library, but at times they had come and gone to their eternal rest before their existence was known of in the capital city.

There are, obviously, good reasons why there have been many failures in newspaper business in a province like British Columbia, where the population is not large and much scattered. Three hundred or four hundred subscribers for a "country" newspaper is not a bad list for this province, and even large papers, like the *Colonist* of Victoria, have a ridiculously small subscription list in proportion to the influence they wield and the amount of money it costs to produce a paper. There are, besides, the high prices of labor, of rent, of paper and printing material. Of course, rates of advertising and subscription are higher somewhat in proportion, and some of your eastern men would grow green with envy if they saw the charges. I have seen as many as eight papers published in a district where there were not that many thousand people altogether. There was, however, always the prospect of making a city, and so the journalist boneyard kept being filled up. It is still filling up as merrily as ever.

Out of the many men who came and went, there were developed some characters. One of them was Mr. John Houston, who first started a little paper in the mountain town of Donald, on the main line of the Canadian Pacific railway, known as *Truth*. Afterwards he printed the *Daily Truth* in the city of New Westminster; and later on dipped into newspaper work in the city of Nelson, where he published the *Miner* and the *Tribune*. He was vigorous in style, democratic in his policy, was more or less oblivious to popular opinion as to his language or the cut of his clothes. He always invariably spelt Mr. with a small "m." As a consequence he became popular with the miners and others who adjured "biled shirts" and fine speech. He acquired considerable property, became mayor of the city, and was elected several times to the Provincial Legislature. Circumstances finally went against him, and he tried his fortune as a printer in Goldfields, Nevada. He is now printing a small newspaper, as virile and as spicy as ever, at Prince Rupert, the proposed terminus of the Grand Trunk Pacific. This he managed to do despite the efforts of the company to dislodge him, and is succeeding. There was another man who came from Petrolea, one of the Lowery Brothers, I believe,

who published the Petrolea *Topic*, of a different stamp
from Houston, but not less remarkable in his way.
When I first knew him he was running a little news
stand at Nelson. Subsequently he blossomed out as an
editor, publishing at various times papers at New
Denver, in the Slocan country, at Lardeau, at Kaslo,
at Greenwood, Nelson, Fernie, and probably elsewhere. His best-known paper was the New Denver
Ledge, somewhat after the fashion of the *Eye-Opener*,
of Calgary. Lowery, if vulgar at times, was really a
humorist. It was finally forbidden of the mails.
He also published a paper styled the *Claim*, which met
the same fate. He concluded finally that British
Columbia was getting too civilized and he left for some
part of the Pacific coast States. He published a paper
at Kaslo, called the *Claim*, which upon its demise he
placed in mourning, the first page being in the form of a
funeral tablet, bearing an adaptation of the usual
tombstone legend in large letters,—Died, etc., and
concluding with "Let her R. I. P." His next venture,
the Lardeau *Claim*, was not more fortunate, and its
last issue was printed on brown wrapping paper, with
a flaring catch line on the title page—"Busted by
Gosh!" It was these melodramatic effects he delighted
in, and made him more or less famous as an eccen-
tricity in journalism of the "wild and wooly" type.
There are others in the same line, feeble imitators of
Houston and Lowery.

The first paper started in British Columbia was
under the auspices of the late Bishop Demers, the pioneer Catholic missionary episcopate of the North-West
coast, much honoured in the annals of the Oblate

Order, more familiarly known, perhaps, as the O. M. I. In the work of writing and publishing, the Bishop was assisted by the Comte de Garro, a Paris Frenchman, who left his native city during and consequent upon the troubles arising out of the *coup d'etat* of Napoleon in 1851. The Bishop had a plant of old-fashioned French type and old-fashioned printing press, and he was anxious to publish a paper in Victoria, largely devoted to church news. Two numbers were published, and the paper died for want of support.

This was followed, after the rush of 1858, by another paper called the Victoria *Gazette*, started by the firm of Whitten, Towne & Co., who ran it until December of the same year, when it went the way of all things. Shortly after the last named came into life, Frederick Marriott, an Englishman, a resident of California, started another paper, called the "Vancouver Island *Gazette*." It lasted for only a few weeks. Before the end of the year a celebrated character in British Columbia history had acquired the plant of Bishop Demers and commenced the publication of a tri-weekly paper bearing the title of the *British Colonist*, from which the *Daily Colonist* of to-day is a lineal descendant, at least in name. Marriott edited for years the *News-Letter* of San Francisco, and was in many ways a remarkable man—fearless, trenchant, cynical. He lived to be an old man, preserving his tireless faculties and his distinguished appearance to the end. A word about the proprietor of the *British Colonist*, who was to take a prominent place in political affairs, and to achieve an almost world-wide celebrity. His real name was Smith, and he came orginally from

Nova Scotia. Attracted by the mining excitement in California, he migrated thither. While in that State he aspired to a more aristocratic name than Smith, and he had the latter changed by Act of the State Legislature to Amor de Cosmos, literally meaning in a combination of words of three languages "lover of the world." He came very nearly going down to posterity however with a less inviting cognomen. During the passage of the bill through the Legislature, one of the members moved an amendment that his name should be Amor de Muggins, which narrowly escaped being carried. Notwithstanding his eccentricities, of which his changing his patronymic was an evidence, De Cosmos was a strong man, an effective speaker and a vigorous writer. He immediately entered into a campaign in the *Colonist* against the Government of the day, which meant Governor Douglas, and during the next twelve years, through the varying phases of political life of the colony, he was ever prominent and in the firing line of the Opposition. He was one of the first advocates of the union of the colonies of Vancouver Island and British Columbia, and when that was effected in 1866, began an agitation in favor of Confederation with Canada. In 1872, by the turn of events, he became Premier of the Province, but subsequently left the arena of the local House for that of the Dominion. The credit and fame of De Cosmos were greatly enhanced by a story of which he was not the real hero. The story, in brief, is that he made the longest speech on record in an effort to save the settlers of Vancouver Island from ruin threatened through eviction, etc. The facts are that it was a Mr. McClure, a brother editor, who made the speech with which he is credited, and it was to prevent a bill brought down by the Government at the eleventh hour to extend the time in which settlers could redeem land sold for taxes from becoming law, that this unparalleled forensic effort was made. De Cosmos and McClure had bought up a lot of this land at tax sales for practically a song, and as times were hard, it was proposed by the Government to extend the time for redemption twelve months. If the bill were not passed before twelve o'clock the next day it would be inoperative, so the two men in question proposed to talk it out, which they succeeded in doing. McClure spoke sixteen hours, when De Cosmos took up the burden and spoke for six hours. Both were thoroughly exhausted. McClure died six months after from a disease superinduced by the tremendous strain on him.

Leonard McClure, the real hero of the story, was editor of the New Westminster *Times*, printed in Victoria by E. Hammond King. It supported the Government of Sir James Douglas in opposition to the *Colonist*. It was removed to New Westminster and succumbed shortly afterwards. So far as known, his speech, on the memorable occasion referred to, was the longest ever made by any public speaker, and it is almost the irony of fate that he should have been robbed of what credit was due him, and at the same time give his life as a penalty for his indiscretion. The *Daily Times*, the *Telegraph*, the *Express*, the *News*, and the *Standard* followed in quick succession in Victoria. The *Chronicle* was established in 1862 by D. W. Higgins, now the *doyen* of newspaper men on the Pacific coast, and Mr.

McMillan, for many years sheriff. Higgins had previously established the *Chronicle* of San Francisco, sold out and came to British Columbia. In 1866 the *Colonist* succumbed to hard times and sold out to the *Chronicle*, both papers being merged into one under the name of the *Colonist*. Mr. Higgins continued in proprietorship and editorial control until 1888, when he entered the local Legislature for Esquimalt, and sold out and retired from journalism, as he thought, for good. Subsequently, he occupied the position of Speaker during two Parliaments, but eventual'y was defeated in his constituency. During his active period of life he acquired large interests, the greater part of which he lost in investments. Within the last few years, he again, with considerable success, turned his attention to literature. Two of his books of short stories of pioneer life in British Columbia were popularly received. For two years he occupied the position of editor of the Vancouver *World*, but has again retired to devote himself to real estate investmen s. Outside of De Cosmos, Higgins has been the most notable figure who has occupied an editorial chair in this province.

The *Evening Post* was established in 1880 by William McDowell, and lived only a couple of years.

The present *Daily Times* was established about 1884, and has developed into the leading Liberal organ of the province.

One of the men associated with this paper from the commencement, and its principal owner, is now a member of the Dominion Cabinet—Hon. William Templeman, Minister of Inland Revenue. Mr. Templeman, though a vigorous writer when the spirit moves him, never identified himself with the editorial side of the paper, but was contented to look after its business interests, and the political possibilities that lay ahead of him. The *Times* is managed by Mr. John Nelson, and is edited by Mr. Dunn, an ingenious and facile political writer.

Vancouver journalism followed in the line of that of other parts of the province—at first ephemeral. The pioneer newspapers were the *News*, the *Advertiser*, and the *Herald;* one of those was started by the son of the late Hon. William Macdougall. The *News* and *Advertiser* were merged into the *News-Advertiser* under its present control, and the *Herald*—conducted by William Brown, many years a real estate agent of the city—died a natural death. In the fall of 1888, J. C. McLagan, who had been associated with Mr. Templeman on the *Times* of Vancouver, and J. M. O'Brien, editor of the *Colonist*, formed a partnership and started an afternoon paper, the *Daily World*, which has withstood the vicissitudes of hard times and is now a paper of metropolitan pretensions. McLagan was a man of tremendous energy, and though rash and impulsive and often erratic, he built up his paper by shrewd enterprise and hard work. At first Conservative, the *World* became in time the recognized organ of the Laurier Government. Later on the *Daily Province* was started under the guidance of its present managing editor, Mr. Walter Nichol, who came here from the Hamilton *Herald*. The original capital for the enterprise was supplied by Hewit Bostock, now Senator, and was, of course, originally Liberal in its policy. Its success from the first was marked, and it for some time has led all the other papers in the province in point of circulation.

A word about the *News-Advertiser*. Its guiding spirit from the time its original factors were merged has been Mr. Francis-Carter Cotton, now Hon. Mr. Cotton, President of the Council. It has been remarkable as the impress of Mr. Cotton's own mind and handiwork throughout its career. Educated and trained in England, not as a journalist, Mr. Cotton has had a variety of experiences in many parts of the world, in banking, diplomatic service, ranching, railway contracting, irrigation, etc., but throughout it all he preserved the English traditions and spirit, which he imparted to his paper. Consequently from the very first it has been Conservative in tone, non-sensational, clean, reliable, and well edited—a good old-fashioned newspaper, going on without change from day to day, uniform in its dress, and consistent in policy with all previous expressions of opinion.

One other marked figure in journalism and politics was the Hon. John Robson. In the early days he edited the New Westminster *Columbian*, which after many years of a chequered career is still in existence and prosperous under the management of Mr. J. D. Taylor. He was a vigorous writer, a forcible speaker, and a remarkably shrewd politician. For some time he occupied the position of editor of the *Colonist*. During the early survey days of the Canadian Pacific Railway he was receiver for the Mackenzie Government. Having made the boast that several millions of dollars passed through his hands without a dollar sticking, a journalistic contemporary, Mr. Suter, of the New Westminster *Guardian*, in his paper christened him "Honest John," by which name he was familiarly known to the day of his death.   Mr. Robson had a long legislative experience both before and after Confederation.   He joined the Hon. A. E. Davie's Government as Provincial Secretary in 1883, and became Premier on the death of his leader.   In 1892, while in England in connection with the large Crofter scheme of colonization, he met with an accident which, though slight in itself, developed into blood poisoning and speedily death.   He was one of the ablest of British Columbia's public men.

Still another man whose connection with British Columbia journalism is worthy of mention was Mr. Henry Lawson, who with rare discrimination and good judgment was editor of the *Colonist* from 1888 until 1897.   Coming originally from Prince Edward Island, he spent some time in Montreal, and finally found his way to the coast under engagement.   There have been several editors of that paper since, including the present occupant of the chair, C. H. Lugrin, Hon. F. C. Cotton, D. B. Bogle, and the writer of this article.   Among others who are either now or have been associated prominently with journalism of recent years are: T. L. Grahame, at one time editor of the *Times*, recently deceased, a versatile and brilliant writer; J. B. Ker, now editor of the Vancouver *Province*, and formerly editor of the Rossland *Miner;* J. D. Taylor, managing editor of the New Westminster *Columbian*, formerly of Ottawa and Victoria papers, now a candidate for Dominion Parliamentary honours;

F. J. Deane, M.P.P., managing editor of the Nelson *News*, the leading paper of the interior; J. M. O'Brien, formerly of the *Colonist* and Vancouver *World;* D. M. Carley, for years in the *Province* in one journalistic capacity or another, and now managing editor of the Nelson *Daily Canadian;* C. E. Race, for some years editor and manager of the Rossland *Daily Miner*, at one time editor of the Nelson *Daily Miner;* the Kennedy Brothers, who conducted the New Westminster *Columbian* for a considerable period; John C. Brown, now warden of the penitentiary, who was editor of New Westminster papers at various times, postmaster of New Westminster, and a member of the Legislature and of the Dominion Fisheries Commission; C. Gregg, assistant editor of the *Daily Colonist*, and for a period editor of the Nelson *Miner* and the Rossland *Miner* and Victoria *Globe;* E. Jacobs, editor of the British Columbia *Mining Record* and correspondent of several leading mining papers, who has the distinction of being the best informed and most reliable writer on mining matters on the coast: C. H. Gibbons, a facile writer, for years associated with the *Colonist* and correspondent of various newspapers; C. H. Lugrin, already referred to, a barrister by profession but a journalist by instinct; Gordon Smith, of the *Colonist*, who made a reputation for himself as war correspondent during the Japanese War, and is a shrewd story writer; W. Blakemore, editor of the *Week* and of the *Westward Ho!* magazine, a particularly bright and effective writer; A. H. Scaife, original founder of the *Province*, a man rarely gifted as a journalist, who contributed materially to the transformation in politics which took place during and subsequent to the time he occupied the editorial chair; Mart Egan, for some time city editor of the Victoria *Times*, for a time very prominent in the Associated Press service, and now editor of the Washington *Star*; Geo. Denny, who served on both the *Times* and *Colonist*, and who is now second in command of the Associated Press in London, Eng.; George Norris, who established, and for many years conducted, the Manitoba *Free Press*.

These are a few of the men whose names come to mind without special reference to order or merit.

There have been frequent collisions between the newspaper press and the courts in consequence of complaints of libel, etc., and on three occasions the press came into collision with the Legislature. On one occasion, in 1861, Mr. De Cosmos of the *Colonist* was brought up for a libel on Mr. Speaker Helmcken, now Hon. Dr. Helmcken, and was arrested by the Sergeant-at-arms, and while the Legislature deliberated what was to be done, he apologized and was liberated.

On another occasion the proprietors of the *Chronicle* were charged with libel on G. E. Dennes, member for Salt Spring Island, and were debarred for one week from sending reporters to the Gallery.

The third occasion was when the Kennedy Brothers (the *Columbian*, New Westminster) were arraigned, fifteen or sixteen years ago, for libel on members of the Legislature. They were arraigned at the Bar, and, refusing to apologize, sentenced to be imprisoned by the Speaker, Hon. Mr. Higgins, until the Legislature had been prorogued. This it did in the course of a day or two, and they were liberated by the Speaker's order.

The first cylinder press was placed in operation in the *Colonist* office in the summer of 1863, and steam was first applied to a printing press in the same office in 1876.

Among the comic papers that have attempted an existence were the *Scorpion* and the *Comet*, two lively but short-lived journals, the later of which was promoted by Mr. John Fannin, the founder and late curator of the Provincial Museum, who, by the way, was an effective writer on natural history subjects.

There were a number of other papers of evanescent character, such as the *Telegram* and *Mail* and *Courier*, of Nanaimo, the *Daily Telegram* of Vancouver, and others almost too numerous to mention here, in various parts of the province. The *Mainland Guardian*, owned by Mr. Suter, was published weekly in New Westminster for a number of years, and was succeeded in 1890 by the *Daily Truth*, and subsequently changed to the *Ledger*, for some years defunct.

Donald, Steveston, Mission City, Surrey, Lardo, Wardner, New Denver, Sandon, Fort Steel, Silverton, Slocan City, Trail, Union, Essington, Three Forks, etc., etc., in recent years each had its whilom journalistic mouthpiece.

At the present time journalism is well represented in the province, and, speaking generally, the press of British Columbia is vigorous and well conducted. Taking the leading daily newspapers, it would be difficult to find in the whole of Canada, having consideration for the size of their respective constituencies, their parallel in size, enterprise, and general efficiency. The Vancouver and Victoria papers especially compare favourably with, if they do not surpass, the largest and best of the Western Canadian papers.

R. E. GOSNELL.

INDEX

Officers:
CANADIAN PRESS ASSOCIATION
1859 to 1908

1859

Meeting for Organisation at Kingston, September 27th, and Toronto, February, 1860

W. Gillespy........President.
J. G. Brown........1st Vice-Pres.
Josiah Blackburn...2nd Vice-Pres.
Thomas Sellar.....Sec.-Treas.
D. McDougall......Hon. Sec.

George Sheppard....
James Seymour....
James Somerville... ⎬ Executive Com.
Thomas McIntosh....
John Jacques.......

1860

Second Annual Meeting at Hamilton, September 28th.

W. Gillespy........President.
D. Wylie...........1st Vice-Pres.
D. McDougall......2nd Vice-Pres.
Thomas Sellar.....Sec.-Treas.
J. E. P. Doyle.....Hon. Sec.

C. J. Hynes........
A. McLachlan......
James Somerville... ⎬ Executive Com.
Josiah Blackburn...
W. G. Culleden....

1861

Third Annual Meeting at London in September.

W. Gillespy........President.
D. McDougall......1st Vice-Pres.
Rufus Stephenson...2nd Vice-Pres.
Thomas Sellar.....Secretary.
J. E. P. Doyle......Hon.-Sec.

J. G. Brown........
D. Wylie...........
M. Coldwell........ ⎬ Executive Com.
A. McLachlan......
J. W. McLean......

1862

Fourth Annual Meeting at Toronto, September 23rd, and Hamilton, November 28th.

D. McDougall......President.
D. Wylie...........1st Vice-Pres.
Thomas White......2nd Vice-Pres.
Thomas Sellar.....Secretary.
M. Bowell.........Hon. Sec.

W. Gillespy........
J. Young..........
J. A. Campbell..... ⎬ Executive Com.
W. T. Cox.........
R. E. O'Connor.....

1863

Fifth Annual Meeting at Toronto, November 20th.

D. Wylie...........President.
Thomas White......1st Vice-Pres.
M. Bowell.........2nd Vice-Pres.
Thomas Sellar.....Secretary.
J. A. Campbell......Hon. Sec.

A. McLachlan......
James Seymour.....
W. Wallace........ ⎬ Executive Com.
George McMullen...
W. T. Johnson......

1864
Sixth Annual Meeting at Belleville, November 24th.

Thomas White......President.	D. Wylie............
M. Bowen..........1st Vice-Pres.	T. Messenger........
Thomas Sellar......2nd Vice-Pres.	J. Somerville........ } Executive Com.
J. A. Campbell......Sec.-Treas.	A. J. Belch..........
W. T. Cox.........Hon. Sec.	J. Laing............

1865
Seventh Annual Meeting at Brockville, September 6th.

M. Bowell..........President.	T. White............
Thomas Sellar......1st Vice-Pres.	D. Wylie............
J. A. Campbell......2nd Vice-Pres.	John Siddons.. .... } Executive Com.
W. T. Cox.........Sec.-Treas.	J. Somerville........
W. Buckingham....Hon. Sec.	W. M. Nicholson....

1866
Eighth Annual Meeting at Montreal, August 22nd.

Thomas Sellar......President.	E. Jackson.........
J. A. Campbell......1st Vice-Pres.	W. N. Nicholson...
W. T. Cox.........2nd Vice-Pres.	A. J. Belch......... } Executive Com.
W. Buckingham....Sec.-Treas.	C. B. Robinson.....
S. I. Jones.........Hon. Sec.	R. Romaine........

1867
Ninth Annual Meeting at Goderich, August 7th.

J. A. Campbell.....President.	W. M. Nicholson....
W. T. Cox.........1st Vice-Pres.	C. H. Hull.........
Robert Boyle.......2nd Vice-Pres.	J. McLagan........ } Executive Com.
E. Jackson.........Sec.-Treas.	J. Hogg............
A. J. Belch.........Assistant Sec.	J. Cameron........

1868
Tenth Annual Meeting at Collingwood, July 10th.

Wm. Buckingham...President.	R. Mathison........
Robert Boyle.......1st Vice-Pres.	A. McLean.........
W. M. Nicholson....2nd Vice-Pres.	J. K. Mason........ } Executive Com.
E. Jackson.........Sec.-Treas.	J. Cameron........
H. Hough.........Assistant Sec.	C. B. Robinson.....

1869
Eleventh Annual Meeting at Cobourg, July 20th.

D. Wylie...........President.	R. Mathison........
J. Cameron........1st Vice-Pres.	W. Gillespy........
A. J. Belch.........2nd Vice-Pres.	W. Halley......... } Executive Com.
E. Jackson.........Sec.-Treas.	W. Buckingham. ..
J. Somerville.......Assistant Sec.	J. S. Gurnett.......

1870

Twelfth Annual Meeting at Brantford, July 19th.

E. Jackson.........President.
J. Somerville.......1st Vice-Pres.
A. McLean.........2nd Vice-Pres.
W. Buckingham....Sec.-Treas.
A. J. Belch.........Assistant Sec.

R. Matheson........⎫
W. R. Climie.......⎪
R. Matheson........⎬ Executive Com.
J. Parnell..........⎪
W. Gillespy........⎭

1871

Thirteenth Annual Meeting at Toronto, July 18th.

James Somerville...President.
Rev. W. F. Clarke...1st Vice-Pres.
E. Miles..........2nd Vice-Pres.
R. Matheson.......Sec.-Treas.
H. Hough.........Assistant Sec.

W. Gillespy........⎫
E. Jackson.........⎪
A. MacLachlan.....⎬ Executive Com.
M. Bowell.........⎪
J. Smith..........⎭

1872

Fourteenth Annual Meeting at Bracebridge, July 10th.

John Cameron.....President.
J. Innes...........1st Vice-Pres.
W. R. Climie.......2nd Vice-Pres.
H. Hough.........Sec.-Treas.
J. G. Buchanan....Assistant Sec.

Rev. W. F. Clarke..⎫
J. Smith...........⎪
T. Messenger.......⎬ Executive Com.
W. H. Hacking.....⎪
E. Jackson.........⎭

1873

Fifteenth Annual Meeting at London, September 24th.

Rev. W. F. Clarke..President.
H. Hough.........1st Vice-Pres.
A. Matheson.......2nd Vice-Pres.
J. G. Buchanan....Sec.-Treas.
John McLean......Assistant Sec.

James Somerville...⎫
E. Jackson.........⎪
P. Burke..........⎬ Executive Com.
John Cameron......⎪
M. Bowell, M.P....⎭

1874

Sixteenth Annual Meeting at Toronto, July 21st.

H. Hough.........President.
A. Matheson ....1st Vice-Pres.
John Smith........2nd Vice-Pres.
J. G. Buchanan....Sec.-Treas.
John McLean......Assistant Sec.

W. R. Climie.......⎫
James Innes........⎪
John Cameron......⎬ Executive Com.
E. Jackson.........⎪
F. J. Gissing.......⎭

1875

Seventeenth Annual Meeting at Hamilton, July 20th.

John Cameron.....President.
C. D. Barr.........1st Vice-Pres..
D. McCullough......2nd Vice-Pres.
J. G. Buchanan....Sec.-Treas.
John McLean......Assistant Sec.

E. Jackson.........⎫
A. Matheson.......⎪
James Somerville...⎬ Executive Com.
W. R. Climie.......⎪
Goldwin Smith.....⎭

1876

Eighteenth Annual Meeting at Toronto, June 30th.

C. D. Barr.........President.	H. Hough..........	
D. McCullough......1st Vice-Pres.	A. Matheson.......	
J. G. Buchanan.....2nd Vice-Pres.	James Somerville...	} Executive Com.
W. R. Climie......Sec.-Treas.	E. Jackson........	
F. J. Gissing.......Assistant Sec.	James Shannon.....	

1877

Nineteenth Annual Meeting at Toronto, August 13th.

James Innes.......President.	H. Hough..........	
James Shannon.....1st Vice-Pres.	John Cameron......	
A. Matheson.......2nd Vice-Pres.	J. B. Trayes.......	} Executive Com.
W. R. Climie......Sec.-Treas.	J. Somerville.......	
F. J. Gissing.......Assistant Sec.	E. Jackson.........	

1878

Twentieth Annual Meeting at Guelph, July 9th.

James Shannon.....President.	H. Hough..........	
Goldwin Smith.....1st Vice-Pres.	N. King...........	
J. B. Trayes.......2nd Vice-Pres.	A. Matheson.......	
W. R. Climie......Sec.-Treas.	E. Jackson.........	} Executive Com.
C. B. Robinson....Assistant Sec.	C. D. Barr.........	
	James Innes........	

1879

Twenty-first Annual Meeting at Kingston, July 22nd.

A. Matheson.......President.	C. D. Barr.........	
J. B. Trayes.......1st Vice-Pres.	H. Hough..........	
E. J. B. Pense.....2nd Vice-Pres.	E. Jackson.........	
W. R. Climie......Sec.-Treas.	James Innes........	} Executive Com.
George Tye........Assistant Sec.	C. B. Robinson.....	
	James Shannon.....	

1880.

Twenty-second Annual Meeting at Toronto, August 5th.

J. B. Trayes.......President.	C. D. Barr.........	
E. J. B. Pense.......1st Vice-Pres.	H. Hough..........	
George Tye.........2nd Vice-Pres.	E. Jackson.........	
W. R. Climie......Sec.-Treas.	James Innes........	} Executive Com.
A. J. Matheson.....Assistant Sec.	C. B. Robinson.....	
	James Somerville...	
	A. Matheson.......	

1881

Twenty-third Annual Meeting at Port Hope, August 2nd.

E. J. B. Pense.....President.
George Tye........1st Vice-Pres.
A. Blue...........2nd Vice-Pres.
W. R. Climie......Sec.-Treas.
A. J. Matheson.....Assistant Sec.

C. D. Barr.........⎫
D. Hough..........⎪
E. Jackson.........⎪
James Innes........⎬ Executive Com.
C. B. Robinson.....⎪
James Somerville...⎪
J. B. Trayes........⎭

1882

Twenty-fourth Annual Meeting at Toronto, August 22nd.

George Tye........President.
C. B. Robinson.....1st Vice-Pres.
G. R. Pattullo......2nd Vice-Pres.
W. R. Climie......Sec.-Treas.
J. B. Trayes.......Assistant Sec.

C. D. Barr.........⎫
H. Hough..........⎪
E. Jackson.........⎪
James Innes........⎬ Executive Com.
H. Smallpiece......⎪
W. Watt...........⎪
E. J. B. Pense......⎭

1883

Twenty-fifth Annual Meeting at Montreal, August 7th.

C. B. Robinson.....President.
G. R. Pattullo......1st Vice-Pres.
J. A. Davidson.....2nd Vice-Pres.
W. R. Climie......Sec.-Treas.
J. B. Trayes.......Assistant Sec.

George Tye........⎫
E. J. B. Pense......⎪
C. D. Barr.........⎪
H. Hough..........⎬ Executive Com.
W. Watt...........⎪
H. E. Smallpiece...⎪
James Somerville...⎭

1884

Twenty-sixth Annual Meeting at Toronto, August 1st.

G. R. Pattullo......President.
J. A. Davidson.....1st Vice-Pres.
W. Watt...........2nd Vice-Pres.
W. R. Climie......Sec.-Treas.
J. B. Trayes.......Assistant Sec.

George Tye........⎫
E. J. B. Pense......⎪
C. D. Barr.........⎪
H. Hough ....⎬ Executive Com.
H. E. Smallpiece...⎪
James Somerville...⎪
C. B. Robinson.....⎭

1885

Twenty-seventh Annual Meeting at Toronto, August 4th.

J. A. Davidson.....President.
William Watt, jr....1st Vice-Pres.
H. E. Smallpiece....2nd Vice-Pres.
W. R. Climie......Sec.-Treas.
J. B. Trayes.......Assistant Sec.

George Tye........⎫
E. J. B. Pense......⎪
C. D. Barr.........⎪
H. Hough..........⎬ Executive Com.
James Somerville...⎪
C. B. Robinson.....⎪
G. R. Pattullo.....⎭

1886

Twenty-eighth Annual Meeting at Toronto, August 5th.

William Watt, jr....President.	E. E. Sheppard.... ⎫
J. J. Crabbe........1st Vice-Pres.	H. P. Moore....... ⎪
A. Pattullo........2nd Vice-Pres.	W. R. Davis....... ⎪
W. R. Climie......Sec.-Treas.	C. D. Barr......... ⎬ Executive Com.
J. B. Trayes.......Assistant Sec.	H. Hough......... ⎪
	J. A. Davidson..... ⎭

1887

Twenty-ninth Annual Meeting at Toronto, August 2nd.

J. J. Crabbe........President.	John Cameron...... ⎫
A. Pattullo.........1st Vice-Pres.	H. P. Moore....... ⎪
E. H. Dewart, D.D..2nd Vice-Pres.	H. Hough.......... ⎬ Executive Com.
W. R. Climie.......Sec.-Treas.	C. B. Robinson..... ⎪
J. B. Trayes........Assistant Sec.	Roy V. Somerville.. ⎪
	William Watt, jr. ⎭

1888

Thirtieth Annual Meeting at Toronto, July 31st.

Also first Winter Session at Toronto, February 22nd, 1889.

E. H. Dewart, D.D..President.	H. P. Moore........ ⎫
D. Creighton, M.P.P..1st Vice-Pres.	A. Pattullo......... ⎪
Roy V. Somerville..2nd Vice-Pres.	Lyman J. Jackson.. ⎪
W. R. Climie......Sec.-Treas.	J S. Brierley....... ⎬ Executive Com.
J. B. Trayes.......Assistant Sec.	J. B. MacLean..... ⎪
	J. C. Jamieson..... ⎪
	J. J. Crabbe....... ⎭

1889

*Thirty-first Annual Meeting at Toronto, July 18th.

Second Winter Session at Toronto, February 14th, 1890.

Roy V. Somerville..President.	H. Hough.......... ⎫
Andrew Pattullo....1st Vice-Pres.	D. Creighton....... ⎪
H. P. Moore........2nd Vice-Pres..	L. G. Jackson...... ⎬ Executive Com.
W. R. Climie.......Sec.-Treas.	J. A. Davidson..... ⎪
J. B. Trayes.......Assistant Sec.	J. S. Brierley....... ⎪
	E. H. Dewart...... ⎭

*This was a purely business meeting, and all papers were deferred until the winter session, held February 14th, 1890, thus making the winter session so important that, after the next year, no further summer sessions were held.

1890-91

Thirty-second Annual Meeting at Toronto, August 5th.

Thirty-third Annual Meeting at Toronto, February 13th.

Andrew Pattullo*... President.	J. B. Trayes........
H. P. Moore........1st Vice-Pres.	T. H. Preston......
J. C. Jamieson......2nd Vice-Pres.	W. R. Climie....... } Executive Com.
J. B. MacLean......Sec.-Treas.	A. F. Pirie.........
J. S. Brierley......Assistant Sec.	Roy V. Somerville..

*The above held office for a year and a half.

1892.

Thirty-fourth Annual Meeting at Ottawa, March 3rd and 4th.

H. P. Moore.......President.	L. W. Shannon.....
A. F. Pirie.........1st Vice-Pres.	T. H. Preston......
P. D. Ross.........2nd Vice-Pres.	Robt. Holmes...... } Executive Com.
J. E. Atkinson......Sec.-Treas.	L. G. Jackson.....
J. S. Brierley......Assistant Sec.	R. L. Mortimer.....
	Andrew Pattullo....

1893

Thirty-fifth Annual Meeting at Toronto, February 9th and 10th.

A. F. Pirie.........President.	J. S. Brierley.......
P. D. Ross.........1st Vice-Pres.	Andrew Pattullo....
T. H. Preston......2nd Vice-Pres.	A. R. Fawcett...... } Executive Com.
J. E. Atkinson.....Sec.-Treas.	L. G. Jackson......
J. B. MacLean......Assistant Sec.	R. Holmes.........
	H. P. Moore.......

1894

Thirty-sixth Annual Meeting at Toronto, February 9th.

T. H. Preston......President.	J. S. Willison.......
L. W. Shannon.....1st Vice-Pres.	R. Holmes.........
J. S. Brierley......2nd Vice-Pres.	C. W. Young....... } Executive Com.
J. B. MacLean.....Sec.-Treas.	W. L. Dingman.....
H. B. Donly.......Assistant Sec.	Andrew Laidlaw....
	A. F. Pirie.........

1895

Thirty-seventh Annual Meeting at Toronto, January 31st.

L. W. Shannon.....President.	C. W. Young.......
J. S. Brierley.......1st Vice-Pres.	J. S. Willison.......
J. B. MacLean......2nd Vice-Pres.	W. S. Dingman..... } Executive Com.
John A. Cooper.....Sec.-Treas.	S. Stephenson......
J. E. Atkinson......Assistant Sec.	A. Laidlaw.........
	T. H. Preston......

1896
Thirty-eighth Annual Meeting at Toronto, February 6th and 7th.

J. S. Brierley.......President.	W. Ireland.........⎫
J. B. MacLean.....1st Vice-Pres.	D. McGillicuddy.....⎪
Robert Holmes.....2nd Vice-Pres.	W. S. Dingman.....⎪
John A. Cooper.....Sec.-Treas.	A. G. F. Macdonald.⎬ Executive Com.
J. E. Atkinson.....Assistant Sec.	R. S. Mortimer.....⎪
	L. W. Shannon.....⎭

1897
Thirty-ninth Annual Meeting at Toronto, February 4th and 5th.

J. B. MacLean.....President.	J. S. Willison.......⎫
Robert Holmes.....1st Vice-Pres.	W. Ireland.........⎪
W. S. Dingman.....2nd Vice-Pres.	Jos. T. Clark......⎪
John A. Cooper.....Sec.-Treas.	D. McGillicuddy.....⎬ Executive Com.
A. H. U. Colquhoun.Assistant Sec.	A. G. F. Macdonald.⎪
	J. S. Brierley.......⎭

1898
Fortieth Annual Meeting at Ottawa, March 10th and 11th.

Robert Holmes.....President.	J. T. Clark.........⎫
W. S. Dingman.....1st Vice-Pres.	L. J. Tarte.........⎪
J. S. Willison.......2nd Vice-Pres.	W. Ireland.........⎪
John A. Cooper.....Sec.-Treas.	D. McGillicuddy.....⎬ Executive Com.
C. A. Matthews.....Assistant Sec.	A. G. F. Macdonald.⎪
	J. B. MacLean.....⎭

1899
Forty-first Annual Meeting at Toronto, February 2nd and 3rd.

W. S. Dingman.....President.	L. J. Tarte........⎫
J. S. Willison.......1st Vice-Pres.	W. Ireland.........⎪
A. G. F. Macdonald.2nd Vice-Pres.	J. T. Clark.........⎪
John A. Cooper.....Sec.-Treas.	D. McGillicuddy....⎬ Executive Com.
C. A. Matthews.....Assistant Sec.	J. F. McKay.......⎪
	Robert Holmes.....⎭

1900
Forty-second Annual Meeting at Toronto, February 1st and 2nd.

J. S. Willison.......President.	A. McNee.........⎫
A. G. F. Macdonald.1st Vice-Pres.	J. T. Clark.........⎪
D. McGillicuddy....2nd Vice-Pres.	A. H. U. Colquhoun⎪
John A. Cooper.....Sec.-Treas.	H. J. Pettypiece....⎬ Executive Com.
A. W. Law........Assistant Sec.	L. J. Tarte.........⎪
	W. S. Dingman....⎭

1901

Forty-third Annual Meeting at Toronto, March 21st and 22nd.

A. G. F. Macdonald..President.
D. McGillicuddy....1st Vice-Pres.
H. J. Pettypiece....2nd Vice-Pres.
John A. Cooper.....Sec.-Treas.
A. W. Law........Assistant Sec.

J. T. Clark.........⎫
A. H. U. Colquhoun.⎪
A. McNee..........⎪
J. W. Eedy........⎬ Executive Com.
Smeaton White.....⎪
J. S. Willison......⎭

1902

Forty-fourth Annual Meeting at Ottawa, February 27th and 28th.

D. McGillicuddy....President.
H. J. Pettypiece....1st Vice-Pres.
John A. Cooper.....2nd Vice-Pres.
J. T. Clark........Sec.-Treas.
M. O. Hammond...Assistant Sec.

A. H. U. Colquhoun.⎫
A. McNee..........⎪
J. W. Eedy........⎬ Executive Com.
A. G. F. Macdonald⎭

1903

Forty-fifth Annual Meeting at Toronto, February 5th and 6th.

H.J.Pettypiece,M.P.P.President.
John A. Cooper.....1st Vice-Pres.
A. McNee..........2nd Vice-Pres.
J. T. Clark........Sec.-Treas.
J. R. Bone........Assistant Sec.

A. H. U. Colquhoun.⎫
D. Williams........⎪
W. E. Smallfield....⎬ Executive Com.
D. McGillicuddy....⎭

1904

Forty-sixth Annual Meeting at Toronto, February 4th and 5th.

John A. Cooper.....President.
A. McNee..........1st Vice-Pres.
A. H. U. Colquhoun.2nd Vice-Pres.
J. T. Clark........Sec.-Treas.
J. R. Bone........Assistant Sec.

D. Williams........⎫
W. E. Smallfield...⎪
J. F. McKay.......⎪
M. A. James.......⎬ Executive Com.
W. Ireland.........⎪
H. J. Pettypiece....⎭

1905

Forty-seventh Annual Meeting at Toronto, February 2nd and 3rd.

Arch. McNee.......President.
A. H. U. Colquhoun.1st Vice-Pres.
J. T. Clark........2nd Vice-Pres.
John R. Bone......Sec.-Treas.
A. E. Bradwin.....Assistant Sec.

J. F. McKay.......⎫
W. E Smallfield....⎪
L. S. Channell......⎬ Executive Com.
D. Williams........⎪
F. H. Dobbin......⎪
John A. Cooper....⎭

1906

Forty-eighth Annual Meeting at Toronto, February 1st and 2nd.

A. H. U. Colquhoun..President.
J. T. Clark.........1st Vice-Pres.
D. Williams........2nd Vice-Pres.
J. R. Bone.........Sec.-Treas.
A. E. Bradwin......Assistant Sec.

J. F. McKay........
W. E. Smallfield....
L. S. Channell...... } Executive Com.
F. H. Dobbin......
C. W. Young......

1907

Forty-ninth Annual Meeting at Toronto, February 7th and 8th.

J. T. Clark.........President.
D. Williams........1st Vice-Pres.
L. S. Channell......2nd Vice-Pres.
J. R. Bone.........Sec.-Treas.
A. E. Bradwin......Assistant Sec.

J. F. McKay......
W. E. Smallfield....
H. B. Donly........
W. M. O'Beirne.... } Executive Com.
C. W. Young......
A. H. U. Colquhoun

1908

Fiftieth Annual Meeting at Toronto, March 5th and 6th.

D. Williams........President.
L. S. Channell......1st Vice-Pres.
J. F. MacKay......2nd Vice-Pres.
J. R. Bone.........Sec.-Treas.
A. E. Bradwin......Assistant Sec.

(elected)
W. E. Smallfield....
C. W. Young......
F. H. Dobbin......
W. M. O'Beirne....
W. J. Taylor......
(ex-officio)
J. T. Clark .... } Executive Com.
H. B. Donly ....
Weekly Section
W. B. Burgoyne....
Daily Section

Membership Roll

of the

CANADIAN PRESS ASSOCIATION

1908

Acton, C. S.............Acton Trade Papers...........Toronto.
Acton, James...........Acton Trade Papers...........Toronto.
Adams, Frank..........Advertiser...................London.
Appleford, L. M........News.......................Seaforth.
Armstrong, W. S. B.....The Pioneer..................Toronto.
Atkinson, J. E.........Star.......................Toronto.
Auger, P. H............Agent Montreal Star..........Toronto.
Auld, J. A.............Echo.......................Amherstburg.

Bastedo, D. E.........Herald.....................Bracebridge.
Bastedo, W. E.........Herald.....................Bracebridge.
Bean, David...........Chronicle-Telegraph..........Waterloo.
Belanger, L. A........Le Progres ....Sherbrooke, P.Q.
Bell, G. J.............Times......................Port Colborne.
Bell, J. J.............Can. Mining Review..........Toronto.
Bengough, J. W........Globe......................Toronto.
Biggar, E. B...........Pulp & Paper Journal........Toronto.
Bilger, W. F...........Agent Montreal Standard.. ..Toronto.
Blackstone, H. T.......Times......................Orillia.
Bole, W. H.............Elgin Sun..................West Lorne.
Bone, John R...........Star.......................Toronto.
Boright, A. T..........News.......................St. John's, P.Q.
Boright, T. A..........Record.....................Sherbrooke, P.Q.
Bourbeau, Aug.........L'Echo des Bois France.......Victoriaville, P.Q.
Bowell, Chas. J........Intelligencer...............Belleville.
Bradwin, A. E.........Reformer...................Galt.
Bragg, H..............Can. Municipal Journal.......Montreal.
Bragg, H. W...........Can. Municipal Journal.......Montreal.
Brennan, F. J..........Standard...................St. Catharines.
Brett, R. R............Free Press..................Essex.
Bridle, A.............Engineering Journal..........Toronto.
Brierley, Jas. S.......Herald.....................Montreal.
Briggs, Rev. W., D.D...Christian Guardian..........Toronto.
Brown, W. J...........Weekly Globe...............Toronto.
Browne, R. H. C.......Nugget....................Cobalt.
Bryan, Claude G.......Journalist..................Toronto.
Burgoyne, Henry B.....Standard...................St. Catharines.
Burgoyne, W. B........Standard...................St. Catharines.

Burrows, Acton........Railway & Marine World......Toronto.
Bywater, H. E........Enterprise-News.............Arthur.

Calkins, H. W.........Standard...................St. Catharines.
Cameron, W. J........Outdoor Canada.............Toronto.
Campbell, A. C.........Hansard...................Ottawa.
Campbell, W. B........Office and Field............Toronto.
Campbell, F. O.........Canadian Courier...........Toronto.
Campbell, Dugald......Gazette...................Almonte.
Canniff, B. E.........Reporter..................Galt.
Carleton, E. M.......Montreal Star.............Toronto.
Carman, T. S.........Ontario..................Belleville.
Carpenter, G. H.......Dairyman.................Peterboro.
Carrel, Frank.........Telegraph................Quebec.
Carswell, R..........Canadian Law Times.........Toronto.
Cave, J. J............Express...................Beaverton.
Cave, John J..........Express...................Beaverton.
Chagnon, A. E........Journal de Waterloo.........Waterloo, P.Q.
Champion, Thos.......Telegram.................Toronto.
Channell, L. S........Record...................Sherbrooke, P.Q.
Charbonnell, L. E......Chronicle.................Cookshire, P.Q.
Chester, Howard......Economist................Shelburne.
Claridge, T. F. E.......Economist.................Shelburne.
Clark, Hugh, M.P.P....Review..................Kincardine.
Clark, J. T...........Saturday Night.............Toronto.
Cliff, W. W..........Central Canadian...........Carleton Place.
Climie, W............Banner...................Listowel.
Colquhoun, A. H. U....Deputy Minister of Education..Toronto.
Copland, John A.......Tribune..................Harriston.
Cook, Fred...........Journalist................Ottawa.
Cooper, John A........Canadian Courier...........Toronto.
Cowan, H. B..........Canadian Horticulturist.......Peterboro.
Cowsert, V. H.........Mirror...................Toronto.
Craick, W. A.........Printer & Publisher..........Toronto.
Craig, W. Logan.......Star and Vidette.............Grand Valley.
Cranston, J. H.........Star....................Toronto.
Creighton, W. B........Christian Guardian..........Toronto.
Crew, T.............Northern Advance..........Barrie.
Crews, A. C...........Epworth Era..............Toronto.
Cromarty, R. R........Canada Law Journal.........Toronto.
Cummings, Mrs W.....Letter Leaflet.............Toronto.
Curran, Robert........News Letter..............Orillia.
Cutting, H. B.........Horticulturist.............Peterboro.

Dale, James..........Guardian.................Toronto.
Davie, A. G..........Tribune..................North Bay.
Davis, W. H..........World...................Beeton.
Davis, W. R..........Advocate.................Mitchell.
Dawson, Wm.........Gazette Review............Parkhill.

Denholm, Andrew......News Tribune...............Blenheim.
Dickson, H. A.........Megantic Gazette...........Rectory Hill, P.Q.
Dillon, R. W..........Journal....................St. Catharines.
Dingman, W. S........Herald.....................Stratford.
Dingman, L. H........Times......................St. Thomas.
Dobbin, F. H.........Review.....................Peterboro'.
Donaldson, A. G......Star.......................Toronto.
Donly, Hal. B.........Reformer...................Simcoe.
Douglas, W. J.........Mail and Empire............Toronto
Downey, J.P., M.P.P....Herald....................Guelph.
Duggan, E. G.........Hansard....................Ottawa.
Dunbar, Robt. C......Hansard....................Ottawa.
Duncan, J. M.........Teachers' Monthly..........Toronto.
Dyas, T. A...........Record.....................Niagara Falls.
Dyas, W. J...........Canadian Druggist..........Toronto.
Dyas, V. W...........Canadian Druggist..........Toronto.

Eastwood, John M.....Times.....................Hamilton
Edmonds, W. L........MacLean's Trade Papers......Toronto.
Eedy, Lorne..........Journal....................St. Mary's.
Egan, Charles........Enterprise.................Wyoming.
Elliott, Fred. B.......Sun.......................Cobden.
Elliott, H. B.........Times......................Wingham.
Elliott, Joseph G......Whig.......................Kingston.
Elliott, W. J.........Chronicle..................Ingersoll.
Ewan, John A.........Globe......................Toronto.

Fawcett, A. R.........Arrow.....................Burk's Falls.
Featherstone, G. W....Star-Transcript............Paris.
Ferrie, Robt. B.......Times......................Hamilton.
Field, Fred. W........Monetary Times.............Toronto.
Findlay, W. A. H......Free Press.................Ottawa.
Finlayson, Hugh........"Journal" Renfrew.........Ottawa.
Fisher, James.........Toronto Agent,.............Toronto.
Fisher, A. M.........Journal of Fabrics..........Toronto.
Fleming, Howard......Sun.......................Owen Sound.
Foley, John..........Sun.......................Orangeville.
Forster, A. S.........Star.......................Oakville.
Fraser, Jane Wells.....East and West.............Toronto.
Fraser, Rev. R. D......Teachers' Monthly..........Toronto.
Fry, W. A............Chronicle..................Dunnville.
Fullerton, J..........Can. Music & Trade Journal....Toronto.

Gagnier, H...........Gagnier's Papers...........Toronto.
Galbraith, Thos.......Mail & Empire.............Toronto.
Garrett, E...........Witness-News..............Bradford.
Gibbard, G. E.........Pharmaceutical Journal......Toronto.
Gibbens, W..........Standard..................Cornwall.

Gilbert, George.........Bulletin....................Toronto.
Giles, J. S.............Watchman..................La Chute, P.Q.
Gillies, Allan.........Watchman-Warder...........Lindsay.
Gillies, D. B...........Canadian Mining Journal.....Toronto.
Given, W. S...........Reporter....................Millbrook.
Good, H. J. P..........World......................Toronto.
Goodfellow, C. A.......Gazette and Chronicle........Whitby.
Goodfellow, J. F.......Free Press..................Midland.
Gordon, C. H..........Jewelers' Journal............Hamilton.
Gorman, F............Observer...................Sarnia.
Graham, Hon. G. P....Recorder...................Brockville.
Graham, Percy M......Recorder...................Brockville.
Grange, E. W..........Mail & Empire..............Toronto.
Grant, S. W..........The Westminster...........Toronto.
Greenwood, W. H......World.....................Toronto.
Gummer, H...........Herald....................Guelph.

Hagey, Jacob.........Gospel Banner...............Berlin.
Hale, C. H...........Packet....................Orillia.
Hallman, H. S........Gospel Banner..............Berlin.
Hammond, M. O.......Globe.....................Toronto.
Hanna, J. B..........Star......................St. Catharines.
Harpell, J. J........Can. Mining Journal.........Toronto.
Harpell, T. W........Can. Mining Journal.........Toronto.
Harper, J...........Echo......................Sundridge.
Harris, W. C. R.......Star......................Toronto.
Harris, Elgin A........Gazette...................Burlington.
Harris, R. B..........Herald....................Hamilton.
Hawke, J. T..........Transcript.................Moncton, N.B.
Haycraft, Miss E. E....Statesman.................Bowmanville.
Heveron, James.......Sentinel...................St. George.
Hocken, H. G.........Sentinel...................Toronto.
Hocken, H. C.........Sentinel...................Toronto.
Hogg, W. A...........Enterprise-Messenger.........Collingwood.
Holmes, R...........New Era...................Clinton.
Holland, J. C.........Journal....................Stanstead, P.Q.
Horton, Albert........Hansard...................Ottawa.
Hunter, G. E. M.......Journal....................Ottawa.
Hurley, J. J..........Canadian Bee Journal........Brantford.
Hutchinson, M. J.......MacLean's Trade Papers......Toronto.

Ireland, W...........North Star.................Parry Sound.
Irving, T. C..........Bradstreet's...............Toronto.
Irwin, William........Chronicle..................Durham.

Jackson, E...........Era......................Newmarket.
Jackson, L. G.........Era......................Newmarket.
Jaffray, J. P.........Reporter...................Galt.
Jaffray, Robert.......Globe.....................Toronto.
Jakeway, H. W........Saturday Night.............Toronto.

James, G. W............Statesman..................Bowmanville.
James, M. A............Statesman..................Bowmanville.
Jeffreys, C. W..........Star........................Toronto.
Johnston, E. W., jr.....Review.....................Bridgeburg.
Jones, Walter W........Gagnier Trade Papers........Toronto.

Keefler, J. K..........Times......................Weston.
Keller, W. H...........Journal....................Uxbridge.
Kerr, J. L.............Standard...................Blyth.
Knowles, C. O..........Telegram...................Toronto.

Laliberte, Wilfrid......L'Echo des Bois Francs........Victoriaville, P.Q.
Lambert, J. A..........Representative..............Mount Forest.
Lance, A. L............Times......................Richmond, P.Q.
Lance, Nye.............Times......................Richmond, P.Q.
Lane, Byron............Press......................Winchester.
Langelier, J. Geo.......Journal de Waterloo..........Waterloo, P.Q.
Langlois, Godfrey......Le Canada..................Montreal.
Lapp, C. A.............Ensign.....................Brighton.
Lawrance, E............Ry. News & Com. Traveller....Toronto.
Leavens, F. N..........Enterprise.................Bolton.
Lebourdeau, H. C.......Record.....................Sherbrooke, P.Q.
Lee, C. H..............Saturday Night.............Toronto.
Le Drew, H. H..........O. A. C. Review............Guelph.
Legge, Geo.............Leader Mail................Granby, P.Q.
Leslie, F. H...........Review.....................Niagara Falls.
Lewis, John............Star.......................Toronto.
Liddell, John..........Times......................North Bay.
Linney, Harry..........Gazette....................Bracebridge.
Livingston, Jas. A.....Independent................Grimsby.
Logie, H...............Record.....................Sherbrooke, P.Q.
Lundy, S. H............Banner.....................Aurora.

MacBeth, Andrew........News.......................Linwood.
MacBeth, Malcolm.......Sun........................Milverton.
Macdonald, A. G. F.....News.......................Alexandria.
Macdonald, J. A........Globe......................Toronto.
MacIntyre, J. R........Herald.....................Dundalk.
MacKay, John F.........Globe......................Toronto.
MacLaren, J. A.........Examiner...................Barrie.
MacLean, J. B..........MacLean's Trade Journals....Toronto.
Maclean, W. F., M.P....World......................Toronto.
Maclean, Wm. D.........Expositor..................Seaforth.
McAdams, Johnston......Canadian...................Sarnia.
McConnell, J. P........Saturday Sunset............Vancouver, B.C.
McDougall, Arch. L.....Can. Implement and Veh. Trade.Toronto.
McGillicuddy, D........News.......................Calgary.
McGillivray, M. W......Toronto Manager Montreal Star.Toronto.
McGuire, B.............Banner.....................Orangeville.

McIntosh, G. J. E.	Standard	Forest.
McIntosh, J. Innes	Mercury	Guelph.
McKay, John A.	Record	Windsor.
McKay, J. D.	Express-Herald	Newmarket.
McKay, K. W.	Municipal World	St. Thomas.
McKay, W. J.	Canadian Baptist	Toronto.
McKerrecher, B. J.	Review	Madoc.
McKinnon, D.	Can. Harness Journal	Toronto.
McKinnon, D. O.	Canadian Manufacturer	Toronto.
McKitrick, A. D.	Banner	Orangeville.
McLean, Hugh C.	Trade Papers	Toronto.
McLeod, James	Gazette	Almonte.
McMahon, T. F.	Liberal	Richmond Hill.
McNee, A.	Record	Windsor.
McTavish, Newton	Canadian Magazine	Toronto.
Marsh, A. W.	Echo	Amherstburg.
Martin, W. T.	Montreal Gazette	Toronto.
Mason, George	Journal	Prescott.
Matthews, C. A.	Hansard	Ottawa.
Matthews, W. C.	Dun's Bulletin	Toronto.
Merrill, Annie	The Prairie	Calgary, Alta.
Merry, W. T.	Guardian	Toronto.
Meyer, N. A.	Leader	Farnham, P.Q.
Milne, W. S.	Money and Risks	Toronto.
Mills, R. E.	Express	Elora.
Mitchell, James	Star	Goderich.
Mitchell, Geo. H.	Post	Hanover.
Monteith, E. C.	Sun	Aylmer.
Moore, H. P.	Free Press	Acton.
Moore, J. E.	Canadian Grocer	Toronto.
Moore, J. M.	Herald	Georgetown.
Morang, Geo. N.	Nor'-West Farmer	Toronto.
Morgan, L. G.	Maple Leaf	Port Dover.
Morrill, V. E.	Record	Sherbrooke, P.Q.
Morrissey, M.	Record	Sherbrooke, P.Q.
Mortimer, R. L.	Free Press	Shelburne.
Moyer, W. A. E.	Journalist	St. Catharines.
Murray, G. M.	Industrial Canada	Toronto.
Murray, J. C.	Can. Mining Journal	Toronto.
Murton, C. A.	Canadian Ready Print Papers	Hamilton.
Neill, J. Stanley	Leader Mail	Granby, P.Q.
Nichol, W. C.	Province	Vancouver.
Nicol, W. Glen	Enterprise	Wyoming.
O'Beirne, W. M.	Beacon	Stratford.
Orr, J. R.	Review	Madoc.
Orr, James A.	Journal	Sudbury.

Panton, Wm..........Champion...................Milton.
Paquette, A. E........L'Industrial.................Shaw'gan Falls, P.Q.
Parkinson, M.........Canadian Teacher...........Toronto.
Parmalee, C. H........Advertiser.................Waterloo, P.Q.
Patterson, J. H. L......Type and Press.............Toronto.
Pearce, C. T..........News....................Toronto.
Pearce, C. G..........Star....................Waterford.
Pelletier, J. E.........Le Journal d'Agriculture......Montreal.
Pense, E. J. B.........Whig....................Kingston.
Perrault, G...........L'Union des Canton de l'est....Arthabaska, P.Q.
Perrault, E...........L'Union des Canton de l'est....Arthabaska, P.Q.
Pettypiece, H. J........Free Press.................Forest.
Phelps, Norman.......Times...................North Bay.
Pierce, E. G..........Record...................Sherbrooke, P.Q.
Planche, R. S.........Record...................Cookshire, P.Q.
Preston, T. H.........Expositor.................Brantford.
Preston, W. B.........Expositor.................Brantford.
Price, H. D...........Express..................Aylmer.

Ramage, C............Review...................Durham.
Rathbone, J. B........Ottawa Journal.............Toronto.
Redditt, J. J..........Methodist S.S. Papers........Toronto.
Reeves, George........Advocate.................Cayuga.
Robertson, J. Sinclair...Telegram.................Toronto.
Robertson, Chas. N.....Journal..................Ottawa.
Robertson, Irving E....Telegram.................Toronto.
Robertson, J. Ross.....Telegram.................Toronto.
Robertson, W. H.......Signal...................Goderich.
Robertson, W. E.......Westminster...............Toronto.
Robertson, Wm........Banner..................Dundas.
Robinson, John R......Telegram.................Toronto.
Roebuck, A. W........Herald..................New Liskeard.
Rook, W. G...........Can. Horticulturist..........Peterboro.
Ross, P. D............Journal..................Ottawa.
Rossie, Melville W.....Advertiser................London.
Rutherford, J. H.......Times...................Owen Sound.
Rutledge, C. W........Standard.................Markdale.
Ryan, J. J............Advertiser................Waterloo, P.Q.

Salmond, James J......Monetary Times.............Toronto.
Sanders, C. H.........Advocate.................Exeter.
Sawle, Chas. H........Progress.................Preston.
Sawle, George R. T.....Messenger................Prescott.
Scroggie, Geo. E.......Mail and Empire............Toronto.
Sears, F. H...........Telegraph.................Welland.
Sears, Thomas H.......Telegraph.................Welland.
Seeley, B. A..........Advance.................Kemptville.
Sellar, R............Gleaner..................Huntingdon, P.Q.
Shants, S. P..........Star....................Toronto.

Sharpin, W. J.........Vidette....................Gorrie.
Shaw, W. A..........Times......................Tilbury.
Shaw, Jean...........Music Journal..............Toronto.
Shurtleff, W. L.........Observer...................Coaticook, P.Q.
Sidey, John J..........Tribune....................Welland.
Simpson, George.......Hansard...................Ottawa.
Sims, Thos. W.........Herald....................Thamesville.
Smallfield, W. E.......Mercury...................Renfrew.
Smallpiece, H. E......Toronto Agent..............Toronto.
Smith, R. Wilson......Insurance Chronicle.........Montreal.
Smith, W. L..........Sun.......................Toronto.
Smith, E. R..........News......................St. John's, P.Q.
Smith, G. P..........News......................St. John's, P.Q.
Snell, Rendol..........Herald....................Marmora.
Snider, Chas..........Telegram..................Toronto.
Southam, Harry S.....Citizen...................Ottawa.
Southam, Wilson M....Citizen...................Ottawa.
Spence, F. S..........Pioneer...................Toronto.
Spence, B. H..........Pioneer...................Toronto.
Spry, D. W. B.........Commercial Publishing Co....Toronto.
Stephenson, S..........Planet....................Chatham.
Stone, C. F...........Expositor.................Perth.
Sutherland, A. E......Transcript.................Glencoe.
Sutherland, F. W.......Municipal World............St. Thomas.

Tarte, L. J..........La Patrie..................Montreal.
Taylor, D. B..........Sentinel Review............Woodstock.
Taylor, W. J..........Sentinel Review............Woodstock.
Templin, J. C.........News Record...............Fergus.
Tessier, G. J.........Le Temps..................Ottawa.
Thomson, J. A.........Journal...................Gananoque.
Thompson, J. H........Post......................Thorold.
Thompson, J. M........Telegram..................Kemptville.
Torrance, T. W........Reporter..................Galt.

Vandusen, H. A........Leader....................Tara.
Van Vleet, P. G.......Implement Trade............Toronto.
Vosper, J. T..........Herald....................Campbellford.

Watson, A. H..........Star......................Creemore.
Waldron Gordon.......Weekly Sun................Toronto.
Walker, Jas. M........Journalist.................Gananoque.
Walker, W. W.........Courier...................Perth.
Wall, Garrett.........Horticulturist..............Peterboro.
Wallis, A. F..........Mail and Empire............Toronto.
Watson, J. P..........Record...................Sherbrooke, P.Q.
Warren, R. D..........Herald....................Georgetown.
Watson, W. J..........Vindicator.................Oshawa.
Webster, A. E.........Dental Journal.............Toronto.

Weld, John............Farmers' Advocate...........London.
Wheaton, J. W.........Farming World..............Toronto.
Wilgress, A. T.........Times......................Brockville.
Williams, D...........Bulletin...................Collingwood.
Williams, W...........Bulletin...................Collingwood.
Williams, Fred. H......Free Press.................Ottawa.
Willison, J. S..........News.......................Toronto.
Wilson, C. A...........North Ender...............Toronto.
Wilson, F. W..........Advertiser.................Petrolea.
Wilson, Geo. H........Post.......................Lindsay.
Wilson, S. Frank.......Wilson's Papers............Toronto.
Wilson, Fred. W.......Guide......................Port Hope.
Wilson, F. Page.......Monetary Times.............Toronto.
Wilson, C. Lesslie......Wilson's Papers.............Toronto.
Wilson, Murray........Wilson's Papers............Toronto.
Wing, M. L.............Evangelius Bote.............Berlin.
Withrow, Florence......Onward....................Toronto.
Woodward, A. C........Banner-News..............Chatham.
Wright, A. W..........Confederate................Mt. Forest.
Wrigley, Weston.......Hardware and Metal.........Toronto.

Young, C. W...........Freeholder.................Cornwall.
Young, J. A............Record.....................Thamesford.
Young, Clarence G......Courier....................Trenton.

Honorary Members

Barr, C. D. Lindsay.
Blue, A., Ottawa.
Bowell, Sir Mackenzie, Belleville.
Boyle, Robert, Picton.
Buckingham, Wm., Stratford.
Cameron, Lud. K., Toronto.
Clark, Dr. D., Toronto.
Crabbe, J. J., Toronto.
Creighton, David, Toronto.
Davidson, J. A., Guelph.
Elliott, R., Brantford.
Gardiner, H. F., Brantford.
Gwatkin, R. L., Toronto.
Hilliard, Thos., Waterloo.
Houston, William, Toronto.
Hough, H., Toronto.
King, John, K.C., Toronto.
McNaught, W. K., M.P.P., Toronto.

Matheson, Hon. A. J., Perth.
Mathison, R., Toronto.
McEwen, W. P., Almonte.
McGuire, W. M., Tillsonburg.
Motz, John, Berlin.
Nicholls, Frederic, Toronto.
Patterson, R. L., Toronto.
Pattullo, G. R., Woodstock.
Russell, S., Deseronto.
Scott, W. C., Napanee.
Shannon, L. W., Kingston.
Somerville, J., Dundas.
Somerville, R. V., London, Eng.
Smith, Prof. Goldwin, Toronto.
Trout, E., Toronto.
Watt, W., Brantford.
Way, B., Hamilton.
Young, Hon. James, Galt.

MURRAY PRINTING COMPANY, LIMITED, TORONTO

8/P

9 781145 779280